SECRETS of The
WREKIN FOREST

C000107915

A 'Green Guide' for thoughtful walkers on Shropshire's favourite hill

Dappled sunlight in the forest.

GEORGE EVANS

Vision Books

By the same author:
Wellington in Old Picture Postcards, European Library, 1987
From Inkwell to IBM, The story of Orleton Park School, 1990
Wellington, A Portrait in Old Photographs and Picture Postcards, S.B. Publications, 1990
Lost Villages of Telford, S.B. Publications, 1991

Dedicated to Naomi and All Friends Around the Wrekin.

First published in 1992 by Vision Books,
15 Market Square, Wellington, Shropshire. TF1 1BU

The road through the Forest Glen.

ISBN 0 9520395 0 8

Typeset, printed and bound by Graphics & Print (Telford) Ltd.,
Stafford Park 15, Telford, Shropshire.

CONTENTS

Ridge track to Hell's Gate.

The Cuckoo's Cup or Raven's Bowl and Gibbon's Coppice.

Primroses.

THE COLOUR PHOTOGRAPHS

The front cover photograph was taken in spring 1992 looking at The Wrekin from the top of The Ercall. Because I do not like the T.V. mast I hid it behind one of the birch trees. This is almost the same view which was used in the geological handbook of 1935, though the view is much changed, Lawrence's Hill being now badly bitten by quarrying.

On the back cover is a shot of a natural bluebell wood in Limekiln Wood, near the path from Steeraway to the old Wellington reservoirs. The combination of bluebells and wood anemones, together with the wild, unkempt trees is, I find, irresistible.

Inside the front cover shows a party of pupils from Orleton Park School in Wellington scrambling on the Cuckoo's Cup. We were on a long walk in the forest to celebrate my retirement.

Also there is an aerial view of the eastern part of the forest, given to me by Francis Brookes. The photograph inside the back cover is of the 'Magic Tree' on the top of the Little Hill at sunset.

INTRODUCTION

TODAY I stood on the summit of The Wrekin, in cool, bright sunshine, and knew that here, above all, was where I wanted to be. Around were lonely woods, painted fields and workaday roads and towns; but here was heather, bilberries and the old hard rocks of my own little mountain. The raven sat gently on a thermal and listened with me to the small birds in the treetops below. The clear air sparkled from Snowdon to the Malverns. It was exciting to be alive in this magical place.

I first went up The Wrekin in a push chair, which must have been a great effort for my father, who had had a bullet through his shin bone in the Great War; I have always been grateful. Most of my life has been spent within sight of the old hill, for which I have maintained a great fondness and I have long been in the habit of saying 'Good morning' each day.

So I wanted to write a book about The Wrekin, though there is a problem with this; will my book make the hill so popular that it will be destroyed? 'Grass grows by inches, but is killed by feet'. Wildlife flourishes best where there are no visitors. The compromise is 'Secrets of The Wrekin Forest', which will describe the popular and the unknown places within the woodlands around The Wrekin and hope that the reader will enjoy and understand enough to preserve the sanctity of what remains of this once great forest.

It was never a primaeval forest; men were here before there were trees, when all was ice and snow, and man remained through the millennia during which tundra became taiga and eventually the broadleaf forest. All this time there have been clearances as our ancestors used the land for their own purposes and we owe it to future generations to pass on at least what remains of the wilder places to them. My grandchildren respect these places as much as my grandparents did; as do my friends.

The forest is very varied, depending upon the underlying rocks, slope and the use to which it has been put. Where there is acid rock the vegetation is very different from the parts where there is limestone; the conifer woods in the west are nothing like the broadleaf areas; dry, well drained, south facing slopes contrast with wet, swampy lands and the places where mining took place long ago are different from newer quarries. This variety is one of the many charms which I have tried to describe; wherever you are it is different just down the track.

There has not been any attempt to organise the reader's walking. This will depend on the walker, the company, the weather, the time available and the mood. Here are some facts, stories, opinions and advice. I hope you enjoy it.

GEORGE EVANS   Wellington under The Wrekin.

*Wellington under
The Wrekin.*

THANKS AND BIBLIOGRAPHY

MOST OF the photographs are my own, taken this year (1992) with a Praktica MTL3 and a Zeiss 50mm lens on Ilford FP4 film processed by Nick Burch, whom I thank. They provided yet another excuse for walking in my favourite places.

I am grateful to the Wrekin Orienteers for the base map and especially to Keith Axon for re-drawing it to fit the book. Julian Langford gave me most valuable advice on the bird life from his thirty years experience of local ornithology. My knowledge of the conservation is thanks to the Chairman of The British Association of Nature Conservationists, my son Paul.

Mr. C.A. Eade, Agent for Raby Estates, has been very helpful with advice on the western forest plantations and Mr. Tony Crumpton, British Coal Opencast Regional Projects Manager, kindly sent me several maps of his latest project.

The University of Birmingham has helped by allowing me to tutor courses at Stirchley Grange Environmental Interpretation Centre, where course members encouraged by questioning almost everything I said.

My wife has inspired, advised and delayed all my work in the most charming way, as have all my family and friends. The forest is only five minutes walk away from home and oak, ash, elm, yew, holly, rowan, birch, elder and hazel grow naturally and happily in my garden, along with wild flowers, many species of birds, frogs, newts, butterflies, dragonflies and other creatures of the woodlands.

I have included with the experiences of nearly seventy years of walking in the woods a great deal of information from books, though this is actually the first book ever written about The Wrekin so far as I know. Below is a list of those maps and books which I have found most useful:

Maps: O.S. Landranger - 127,
                O.S. Pathfinder - 870 & 890
                I.G.S. Geological map 1:25000 SJ60 Telford

Books: Colebourne & Gibbons - Britain's Natural Heritage (Blandford)
                Andrew Morton - The Trees of Shropshire (Airlife)
                Peter Toghill - Geology in Shropshire (Swan Hill)
                S.C.Stanford - The Archaeology of the Welsh Marches (Stanford)
                Andrew Jenkinson - Shropshire Countryside (Minton & Minton)
                Tobin *et al* - The Woodlands of Telford New Town (F.S.C.)
                G.C.Baugh *(ed)* - Victoria History of Shropshire Vol XI (O.U.P.)

There is, however, no substitute for walking, looking, thinking, listening, smelling and wondering. For those occupations you will need a good pair of boots, a waterproof, an inquiring mind and a sense of humour. Have fun!

CONSERVING THE WILDSPACE

TO ME, the Wrekin Forest is extremely important, but why should anyone else be concerned? There are no whales, pandas or elephants to be protected from extinction. No-one has made a television documentary of these woods, let alone a mini-series or a soap; how can it be worth protecting if it is not famous?

Some things are ephemeral; I just swatted a housefly before it infected our food. My neighbours' cats, who stalk birds in my garden, only survive because I respect their owners. Otherwise they would be as ephemeral as the housefly. Most of us will not last long or be remembered. The Wrekin, having survived for millions of years is another matter. Yet it is constantly under threat, both to wildlife and to the very rocks themselves. Mining and quarrying have removed rock; farming, building, tourism and a host of other activities affect wildlife. Conflict is the normal state.

The Wrekin Forest is unique - so are we all. God - or Nature, I can't tell the difference - created us all different, for which we should be grateful. This divorces us from simplistic mathematical theories but makes life more interesting. Whoever said of redwood trees, 'When you've seen one you've seen 'em all', was only demonstrating monumental ignorance. There's a lot of that about!

We are urged to 'think globally, act locally', and we hear from the media of rainforests, deserts and icecaps to be protected. There's global warming, the ozone layer, all manner of major catastrophes, about to inflict themselves on us. In every scenario man is the villain, either in the form of international business or wars or debt-ridden governments. Perhaps with the lessening of the threat of atomic war we need an impending catastrophe to worry about. Or maybe these scares replace fear of the Devil, in whom we no longer believe.

But there is no doubt that things are going wrong, that mankind is responsible, and we ought to do something to halt our slide to destruction and reverse it. Why? Because we all believe in the survival of our own species if not any other. We may favour the protection of cuddly or photogenic creatures but the only reason to protect mosquitoes, rats or bacteria is to conserve our own kind. Our strong instinct - not belief, instinct - to promote the survival of mankind lies behind all our thoughts of conserving the environment from ourselves. Man is the culprit; we are our own worst enemies. James Lovelock has introduced the concept of Gaia, the biosphere as an organisation of living organisms, which has created and controlled the environment, the atmosphere and oceans for its collective benefit. This is true global thinking, a huge and wonderful idea, still being developed but insufficiently publicised as yet. It should be compulsory study for all national and local planners.

Post-industrial resurgence — Birch Coppice, New Works.

David Bellamy's 'Magna Carta Secunda' - an environmental charter signed under the same yew tree as King John's version, 777 years ago, can serve as a useful basis for acting locally. Incidentally, his yew is rather smaller and younger than ours on The Wrekin. Bellamy refers to areas like our forest as Wildspace. He goes on to say, "All Wildspace will be protected, guarded and wherever and whenever necessary managed for the good of all its inhabitants by landowners, local people, Governmental and non-Governmental organisations alike."

I worry about some organisations' management schemes, however. Some local ones are well conceived but others are disasters - they couldn't organise a booze-up in a brewery. If they would only think more of the wildlife and less of profit, voters or their promotion prospects the results would be better. 'Hands off' management allows wildlife to live wild; only people need to be managed. Wildlife networks and tree planting are praiseworthy, but true Wildspace cannot be created. There are always ambitious people who think that, because they have a position or a qualification, like Nanny they know best but this is a very complex Wildspace. Some local dog-walkers are far better informed than the average 'expert'.

There is a theory which suggests that the chief reason why so many Wellington people are fond of these woods is that they were conceived here. It is only a hypothesis. A more likely reason is that for several millennia The Wrekin was a sacred hill to all who lived in its vicinity and the collective tribal memory lingers on. For whatever reason we love The Wrekin.

So, because we love it, let us actively protect and guard this wonderful place against all comers, including well meaning incompetents. The Wildspace includes all the wild things in the woods; blackbirds and worms, badgers and slugs, and in spite of their revolting habits, magpies and cuckoos. Arsonists and litter-louts, rapists and muggers, exploiters and landscape sterilisers should be among those enemies on whose toes we wish the Devil to rain pebblestones, so that we may know them by their limp, as the Wrekin toast goes.

After many years of campaigning for the protection of this Wildspace, 'Secrets of The Wrekin Forest' includes a plea to all its readers to take over the constant vigil needed. Once you know some of its secrets and understand its wonder the reasons will be clear. What to do? Here are some suggestions:
1.   Keep an unblinking watch for any signs of impending change.
2.   Judge each on its total effect on the Wildspace inhabitants.
3.   Act swiftly, decisively and together for as long as it takes. I wish you the best of luck - you will need it!

'Forest City' planting — Telford Central Station.

SECRETS OF THE WREKIN FOREST

Chapter One

THE GREEN ENIGMA

THE WREKIN rises proudly above the surrounding plain, a long wooded hogback with four attendant ridges. One of the first questions it poses is how it came to be there. There are several stories about giants and an equally fictitious one about it having been a volcano. The truth is more amazing than the fiction.

If you ask locally the first answer given usually begins with 'Well, there was this giant . . .' Briefly, the giant had a grudge against the people of Shrewsbury because he had heard they had stolen eels from his trap lower down the Severn. He decided to drown them all by blocking the river with an enormous spadeful of earth. On the way he met a cobbler called Crispin and asked how far it was. Crispin did not want all his customers drowned so he tipped out all the shoes from his sack and said he had worn them out walking from Shrewsbury. The giant decided not to bother with his dam and threw down his earth, which formed The Wrekin.

Arthur Mee, in his book on Shropshire, talks of the ancient fires of the extinct volcano. This is also fiction and I suspect Mee had never seen the county he was writing about.

In the modern geologists' account The Wrekin is formed of very ancient rocks, some volcanic, some plutonic and others sedimentary. The oldest of these were laid down during the Precambrian period, over 600,000,000 years ago, around the latitude of Australia. The land was raised up by a great fault (rather like the well known San Andreas in California). This place has been in deserts, tropical forests (hence the coalfield) and under the ice, though as ice sheets do not move uphill the top was not covered. The fault was active, giving rise to earthquakes and earth movement until around 50,000,000 years ago. There are many smaller faults associated with the main one; the 'geological wall' on Queensway gives a good graphical illustration of the complexity of faulting in the coal measures.

Around 6,000 years ago, when Britain separated from Europe, the landscape was covered in forest, though even then there were clearings with farms. There had been people on and around The Wrekin before the Ice Age, but there are no traces of them. These people were hunter/gatherers, and from what we know of Inuit (Eskimo) life recently it is reasonable to suppose that it would be quite possible for humans to survive during Ice Age times. The story of the mammoths found a few years ago makes it clear that before the forest there were meat

The Wrekin hogback from May plantation.

The Ercall from the beech avenue.

supplies to be had. After the last Ice Age (there were several) the earth gradually warmed, going through tundra and coniferous forest until at last broad-leafed forest became the natural vegetation as it is today.

The first local farmers, of the New Stone Age, had only simple light ploughs; they would not have been able to tackle the heavy clay lands and it is safe to assume that they farmed only the light sandy soils to the north and left most of the claylands as forest. That is not to say that they left the forest alone - far from it. There were animals and birds worth the trouble of hunting, not to mention timber for building and fuel. They also raised stock and may have used some of the land too heavy to plough for pasture.

So although in pre-historic times The Wrekin Forest was much bigger and denser than it is now there was never a 'primaeval forest' before man; man came before the forest. Its greatest extent was from where Shrewsbury is now to about Newport; from the Weald Moors in the north to the Severn in the south. On a fine day a visitor who climbed The Wrekin to look around would have seen trees in most directions, with some smoke drifting up from fires around Wellington, Walcot and Wroxeter. One thing has not changed - The Wrekin is a fine landmark and the best place from which to spy out the land.

Bronze Age people have left their graves in the Willowmoor, though these were plundered last century and the contents taken to Shrewsbury. They built the hillfort on the top, which was enlarged and rebuilt in the Iron Age. This will have been the first town in the area, a tribal headquarters and an important religious site. We will examine the 'sacred rocks' later on. From this town a large area was governed until the arrival of the Romans, when the capital was transferred to the New Town (what is new about new towns?) at Viroconium Cornoviorum, or as we now call it Wroxeter. Both were clearly named after The Wrekin.

The Celts used the forest for charcoal for their iron founding, and this was continued until Abraham Darby used coke instead. Actually charcoal was produced here until Grooms of Wellington introduced a large industrial kiln in the 1930s, and many of the older trees still show the signs of coppicing for charcoal by Alf Wilkes and his men. There are also many small platforms in the woods where you can scrape away the leaves in winter and find evidence of charcoal burning underneath.

Most of the soil, apart from on the top of the ridges, is formed of debris brought by the ice sheets. It has become soil due to exposure to weathering and with the help of micro-organisms whose chemical actions supplemented the ice, rain and wind. Left alone this soil will naturally grow broad-leafed forest, suitable for deer, wild ox, pig, wolves and bears, not to mention the same wide range of birdlife we now enjoy and many smaller creatures such as insects, frogs, slugs and so on. It is hardly a surprise that the Saxons and Normans kept it for a Royal hunting forest.

The Wrekin is still a landmark and a lookout, a hill much loved by all those who know it. There are many places proudly called Wrekin View; the District Council is The Wrekin, and so used to be the local beer. Our Wrekin Forest is part of an area of outstanding natural beauty, a site of special scientific interest and an Ancient Monument. This, however, does not stop some people trying to nibble away with little development projects, but there are always some locals who will fight to preserve the last remnants of ancient woodland.

A look at a modern map which gives parish boundaries is at first a surprise. The Wrekin is in two separate District Council areas and several parishes. It would make more sense, you might think, to put it all in one parish. Yet when villages were using the forest for grazing, timber and small game it was necessary to give a share to several parishes.

Walking is a natural thing to do on The Wrekin and its associated hills, and there are several public footpaths, described later in more detail. How old are the rights of way? Well, the ridge path must be at least 10,000 years old! Then there is the question of open access; fortunately the owners of the land have never objected, though they would be perfectly entitled to charge anyone who damaged the woodland or interfered with the landowner's reasonable use of his land. For example, I find it most unreasonable to disturb golfers, quite apart from the danger of a very hard ball, and I do not want to be between a pheasant and a man with a gun.

The footpaths are well used, especially the main path from the Forest Glen to the top. One winter weekend we counted the walkers above the Cottage on Saturday and Sunday; there were 600! On another occasion we found at least fifty people between midnight and two in the morning in pouring rain; it was New Year. Yet often one can walk around on the main perimeter track without meeting anyone, even on a fine Sunday.

There are many individual and family customs which have been built up over the years. Mine is not the only family which says 'Good morning' to The Wrekin every day, and I understand that there is a judge who invariably has his Christmas lunch on the top. Someone used to hoist a flag each New Year, and though I noticed it was not there in 1992, there was a large party to drink the toast to 'All Friends Around The Wrekin' at midnight. Orleton Park School has an annual race from school to the top and back for the fifth year (now called year 11) on the day they leave. The record is around forty minutes, which is a very good time by any standards, and most complete the course.

Most of the Wrekin walkers are polite, considerate and friendly - this is, after all the land of 'All Friends Around The Wrekin'. There is little litter away from the car parks. There are two problems, however. The main path is widening and destroying vegetation and some of the

Dappled sunlight on the beeches.

The Ercall and Lawrence's Hill Quarries

horse riders insist on riding over the hillfort gates, cutting grooves in the 2,000 year old walls. The pathways could hardly stand any more pressure, and although in one way one would like to see more people enjoying the walk it makes little sense to destroy such a wonderful place by over-using it.

Away from The Wrekin itself there are far fewer visitors; apart from the north slope of The Ercall, which is owned by the County Council, the rest of the forest is relatively very quiet. Even on the track from Steeraway to The Hatch it is not often that you will meet anyone. In the Short Woods, Limekiln Woods, Black Hayes, Wenlock's Wood, Gibbons Coppice (apart from the Scout Camp) and the Little Hill Woods to meet another person is quite an occasion.

The disused quartzite quarries opposite Buckatree Hotel have become a regular dog walkers' paradise and often are full of geologists, as this is an important outdoor laboratory for their science. Some of the outcrops suffer from geological erosion - erosion by geologists - as samples are taken for study. Within the quartzite was a little gold, but it would be much cheaper to buy from a High Street jeweller than to extract the gold from there.

With its great variety of rocks - ancient volcanics, quartzite, shales, sandstones, limestone and coal measures together with varied slopes, sunlight availability and water retention there are bound to be enormous variations in vegetation. Added to the factors above there is a question of age; some of the land has been little disturbed for centuries and is semi-natural woodland, whilst in other places there has been disturbance since 1990. Planting has also affected vegetation; for example the western end, around the Little Hill, has been planted with conifers which have made the soil much more acidic. Once the Little Hill was called Primrose Hill, but because of the planting there are no primroses now.

At the south of The Ercall, where the only land use has been for grazing, coppicing and charcoal burning, are many bluebell woods. These not only look and smell wonderful, they are a unique ecology, peculiar to Britain, and must be protected at all costs. Bluebell woods are more important to Britain than any exotic species and more worthy of our protection. Some would say that bluebells should have priority over such new inventions as parliament or churches.

In some of the old meadows near the woodlands and on the limestone areas are orchids and other lime-loving plants. There is a wonderful range of mushrooms, toadstools and other fungi to be seen in the autumn and picked and eaten if you know what is good for you - but otherwise left alone, for some are deadly poisonous. There were Polish people who arrived after the last World War who are experts and have been seen taking advantage of their knowledge, but most of the 'locals' leave fungi wisely alone.

Many of the older oaks have been coppiced, sometimes several times. It is very difficult, perhaps impossible, to make a sensible guess at their age, for they may well be several hundred years old. Free standing trees are easier to date, they will be about sixty or seventy years old, and were deliberately planted when Grooms bought all the timber in the forest. Any younger trees, except in the conifer plantations, are selfsetters. This will include any trees not normally used commercially, such as birch, rowan or holly. A rule of thumb for tree ages is to take the diameter at shoulder level in inches, which should be the age in years.

Dead trees and branches are an important factor in the ecology, as they provide food for insects, which in turn feed birds. Where all the trees are healthy there will be no woodpeckers. There has been talk of 'managing' the woodland, but that usually means tidying it up. If that is to be like the treatment given to Apley woods by the Development Corporation, which reduced the bird species by a third we must resist the temptation. Have you ever heard of anyone walking in woodland being struck by a falling tree branch?

There were once stands of elms, some planted for aircraft manufacture, but they have all (I think all) been killed off by Dutch elm disease. However there is a young one in my garden and one day they will be back. Birch, 'the white lady of the forest', grows quickly and easily almost anywhere and is colonising some of the newly exposed quarry faces. Holly is plentiful near water; this winter (1991/2) there were few berries. Yew grows slowly and it may be that a yew grove under the Needle's Eye is the oldest plant in the forest.

The undergrowth is even more varied than the tree cover. The Ercall and part of The Wrekin, where the underlying rocks are acidic have bilberry and heather, in places with beautiful fescue grasses, which are fine and soft. Lime-rich soils have their own ecology. In at least one of the many wetlands you will find horsetails, a terrible trouble to a formal gardener but an interesting wild plant, as it is a survivor from the Carboniferous age when it grew to tree height and died to form coal. In the wetlands are also many ferns, moses and lichens.

Wild flowers are in abundance except under the conifers, and even here they flourish in glades and near paths. Recently disturbed soil is rapidly colonised by rosebay willow herb (fireweed), dandelions or other quick growing, multiseeded plants which can take early advantage, but these are soon shouldered out by stronger but slower species. A walk in the forest in spring will bring you to little clumps of primroses, violets, bugle, archangel, celandine or campion, all worth stopping to look at. Unless, that is, you are in a hurry; in which case perhaps you should not be in the forest at all!

So far we have discussed the last remains of the forest. The countryside around has been described - by myself if by no-one else - as like a palimpsest. This is an ancient parchment

Wood anemones in Limekiln Wood.

Wellington from The Ercall.

which has been used and re-used many times, bearing the marks of former writing. The land that was once woodland has been cut and farmed, some of it since pre-historic times. From the top of the hill are seen miles of fields punctuated by villages and small woods. There are bright yellow oilseed rape fields, poppies where an old pasture has been ploughed or dark green sugar beet. There are still hedges in most places and narrow roads, though to the east is another picture altogether.

I cannot do better than to urge the reader to go and look at this palimpsest of a landscape with its marks made by prehistoric man; by Celts, Romans, Saxons, Normans and most of those who have inhabited it, Including what is happening now. There is no finer place anyway than The Wrekin. Am I prejudiced? Perhaps a little, but see for yourself.

Telford New Town has been developed on a part of the forest which had for centuries been small towns and villages, growing naturally as industry came and went and changed. This is the east Shropshire coalfield, sometimes called the Coalbrookdale coalfield. Here it was found long ago that the rocks under the soil were worth more than the soil itself, because there were coal, ironstone, fire- brick- and tile-clay and limestone which could make fortunes for industry. It was not all Abraham Darby and Thomas Telford, though they certainly had their part; for more information see 'Lost Villages of Telford'.

Now the eastern area is covered in buildings and roads, as densely packed with houses and factories as it once was with trees. Yet the trees are still there, in gardens and along the roads, old trees and newly planted ones. Telford is advertised as 'Forest City' with some justification. It has been said without justification - that before the area became a new town all was gloom and doom, pit mounds and dereliction. In fact a large proportion of the new building has been on good farmland which before the designation of Telford was highly productive.

Much of the old forest area has been 'improved' which has usually included drainage work. In particular the Weald Moors, once wild wetlands, suitable only for fishing, wildfowling and hunting, have had drainage schemes imposed upon them over many centuries. Now the pools, swamps and alder carr left behind by the ice age have all been tidied up and are farmlands. The last phase of this drainage has been done by the Development Corporation to build factories at Horton and Hortonwood. Before them were the Leveson-Gower (Marquess of Stafford and Duke of Sutherland) family, who turned the moors into farmland and made a fortune to add to the one they made by exploiting the mineral wealth and industries in the coalfield.

Where there have been disturbances to the soil and vegetation, whether by quarrying, mining, road building, drainage, farming or gardening, the forest cover tries to recolonise the land. Given the slightest chance the natural vegetation will return. It may take time, and there will be an interim period in which the ground cover can hardly be recognised as broadleafed forest or anything like it. But inexorably, unless there is constant effort to prevent it, the forest will be back. Gardeners will know this from experience.

Some of the interim regimes can be seen in old pit-mounds and other spoil-heaps. Unfortunately 'Authority' finds it difficult to leave these places alone, and they are tidied up with the result that they become sanitised and boring instead of an exciting view of a struggle between man's pollution and nature's efforts to put things right. Although it was official policy to allow more mature regeneration, where oak and ash trees had developed, what was contemptuously termed 'scrub', which was only an earlier stage in the same struggle, was usually condemned to be bulldozed and grassed. Yet some of the 'scrub' was beautiful, full of flower-rich meadows, hawthorn, rowan, gorse, broom, not to mention birds and butterflies.

The people of The Wrekin Forest have paid a higher price for Telford New Town than the planners ever dreamed. Perhaps if there had been real consultation with the locals it may have been done more sympathetically. But as the early planners and organisers must have realised, with full local consultation and participation it would have taken more time and might never have happened at all. In the event there was very little notice taken of any other opinions and whatever was decided in Whitehall was done efficiently and swiftly here. Central government paid £600,000,000 which is over £10,000 per new person brought in, and east Shropshire was greatly changed.

But let us say a good word for Telford; there has been a very great number of trees planted, in every possible, available space. Some would say that they are the wrong trees, or that they are in the wrong place, but at least there are a lot of trees. There are trees and shrubs in most gardens too; whether there is room or not, most of the private houses in Telford have at least one or two. My own garden contains a dozen trees, though when they are all grown there will be nothing like enough room; I hope that the house, rather than the trees will be pruned.

Many of the old towns and villages of the coalfield betray their origins as forest clearances by names ending in the suffix -ley, as for example Hadley, Dawley, Madeley, Ketley and also Malinslee and Leegomery. They were enclaves in the old Wrekin Forest, though how much the clearing was agricultural and how much was industrial must have varied from place to place and from time to time. Where there was outcrop iron ore might well be the first of the clearings, though this would give way to mining when the surface ore was used up, and with charcoal from the forest there would be iron working. Together with the small scale industries like these would be smallholdings and a little poaching on the side.

Southwards many of the fields are quite small between the hills and the river, where the land

Quartzite strata and resurgent vegetation at the Ercall Quarries

South-west from the Needle's Eye, a palimpsest.

slopes steeply down from 1,350 feet to just over 200. The landscape is dominated by the electricity power station at Buildwas, with its tall chimney and pink cooling towers, a significant source of pollution. This feeds on coal from a specially preserved local railway and from the many open-cast coal mines which are extracting the last remains of coal from the more shallow or western part of the coalfield. These lands have already been mined, often using bell-pits or adits, but modern methods are able to exploit thinner seams and the spaces between the old pits.

The Severn, sprawling in meanders past Leighton, is forced into the narrow gorge which begins at Buildwas and made to take life more seriously. Even there it is not so fast, for it falls only a foot a mile before it enters the sea. Beyond the river are the wooded hills of Wenlock Edge, with the Brown Clee and Titterstone Clee, bristling with radar and radio masts looking over the top. Often there are floods along the river, when the 'crooked S' meanders at Leighton disappear under water.

Little Wenlock, apparently a quiet well heeled rural/ commuter village, hides more coal, iron and limestone mining under its calm exterior than might be expected at first glance. There has quite recently been open-cast working and more is planned. This is a very old settlement and may well have been continuously occupied since Iron Age men needed iron ore, say 2,500 years ago.

Northwards there is no coal, just good agricultural land, well farmed for centuries. Two large plumes of smoke indicate the presence of the sugar-beet factory and the creamery. Sugar beet was introduced just before the second world war with the help of experts from Czechoslovakia. During the 'campaign' the factory is extremely busy and imports temporary labour. Recent expansion here and at the Crudgington creamery, famous for developing Limeswold cheese, has been helped by European Community funds. The M54 motorway and its new extension in the dual carriageway A5 cut across the farmlands; it is to be hoped that landscaping and tree planting will soften their impact. There is also a chemical works, developed in a wartime optical factory on Overley Hill, just another landscape blot which would, one would hope, never have planning permission nowadays.

To the west are fields, farms, villages and clumps of trees where the old woodlands once were. Beyond is the Severn, the hills of south Shropshire and the more distant mountains of Wales. On a fine day, 'High the vanes of Shrewsbury gleam, islanded in Severn stream,' as Houseman said, and he is still right. The general impression in this, as in every direction except east, is of farmscape with many trees. Trees stand in the hedgerows, beside the roads and lanes and often in the middle of fields too. Even in the east there are trees; Wellington has thousands, mostly in gardens, and the estates of the new town are gradually beginning to green as the new planting prospers. Factories and schools, offices and homes, all seem to need to plant a few trees for screening, softening and enhancing their environment. This is very much as it should be, for after all, this is still a part of the ancient forest of The Wrekin.

The view from the top is never the same two days running and there are times when it is almost impossible to see more than a few feet and at other times Snowdon is quite clear. Recently I was asked how many counties could be seen (it used to be 17); we decided to settle for Shropshire, Cheshire, Derbyshire, Staffordshire, West Midlands, Worcestershire & Herefordshire (one or two as you please), Powys, Clwyd and Gwynedd; more may occasionally be possible (I have seen barrage balloons at Liverpool, but not since 1945.)

The Wrekin's oak woodlands are rich in birdlife; in summer roding woodcock are seen at dusk, also nesting wood warbler, redstart, pied flycatcher in good numbers. All three species of woodpecker nest, along with blackcap, garden warbler, whitethroat and chiffchaff. Sparrowhawk are common and they and kestrels are seen hunting. In clearings linnets, yellowhammer and many species of warblers nest. Tawny owls nest and probably buzzards too. Flycatchers, warblers and redstart nest within 100 yards of the main track. In winter siskins and redpolls, sometimes in large flocks feed on larch cones and parties of titmice accompanied by goldcrests.

What remains of this once great forest is a group of woodlands around The Wrekin and its tributary hills. It is much shrunken from its former extent but still a wonderful place in which to be, well worth studying and the subject of the rest of this book. It exists in three dimensions of space and the extra dimension of time. The woods are extremely varied in vegetation types, in underlying rocks and soils and in their history and pre-history; also in their modern uses.

The Wrekin Forest is best seen on foot, and at a leisurely pace. The best weather is dappled sunshine, but it is wonderful at dawn or sunset, in the snow, or the mist, or the rain, or drizzle, sleet, wind, thunderstorm - any weather and any time of day or night. One thing is certain, each time it will look or sound or smell or feel different from the one before, full of magical places which are always changing.

Spring in the Ercall Woods.

Chapter Two

SUMMIT

W E NOW go and see for ourselves, retracing the footsteps of our ancestors, the finest view (in the world to some of us) from the top of The Wrekin. The usual - to many people the only - way to the top is from the Forest Glen up the rough winding track. Vehicles use this way to service the TV station; they are supposed to lock the gates behind them, but this never happens. Fortunately there are very few vehicles, and for the sake of walkers they are to be discouraged.

At the foot there used to be an old woman who sold what she called 'Weekie wock made out of sugar and honey', but no-one sells rock any more. Later there were 'stop me and buy one' ice cream sellers. Now there is only a public lavatory, very useful in summer but closed in winter, in spite of the thousands of people who would use it.

Try to stay on the established paths; many birds nest on or very close to the ground and it is easy to step on a nest without knowing. Interfering with a nest is not only unthinkable but illegal. Before 10 a.m. is the best time for watching birds, especially in May and June. Binoculars are necessary and something to sit on is useful; so is patience! This path is an excellent place to watch feeding birds as caterpillars fall from trees and are quickly disposed of.

The track is an official public footpath; it has been used for several thousand years so it could hardly not be. It is not particularly steep; for those who need a challenge there are more direct ways, mostly up scree. Just below the Wrekin Cottage, sometimes called the Halfway House, another track goes straight on round the perimeter but we turn right past the cottage. This is the only house on The Wrekin. At the corner are the remains of old pig styes which supplied the ham for ham and egg meals when the cottage was a major tourist attraction.

There also used to be 'swingleboats' and donkeys. It was a tradition to pause to order supper from Miss Birrell on the way up and eat it with a bigger appetite on the way down. Recent residents kept goats which had a habit of eating anything, especially the notes of children in school parties. Now there are no refreshments to be had, as it is a private house.

Just above the cottage the track becomes a ridge walk, with many false dawns which appear to be the top. On the ridge the forest is clear and we rise above it. From here the dawn chorus is below; an interesting experience. The views are marvellous, especially back over Wellington.

The Halfway House in its hey-day.

Approaching Heaven's Gate.

Victorian families used to leave grandparents at the Forest Glen, less fit adults and small children at the cottage and only the fittest made the top. We may well find pensioners as well as children, joggers, families, orienteers, locals, foreigners, horseriders and mountain bikers. By far the best maps of the area are made by the local orienteering club.

In a small dip below the first hillfort entrance used to be a stone marking the boundary between the Orleton estate and the Raby lands owned by Lord Barnard; goodness knows where it has gone. The ownership is clear enough, however, as only the Raby estate grows commercial conifers and Orleton keeps to natural woods and leaves them alone.

Here or hereabouts was, in the 'good old days', the scene of annual fights between colliers and yeomen for the top of The Wrekin. It was part of a trade fair which mixed commerce, religion and drinking. These fights became so bloody that they were stopped - by withdrawing the beer which promoted them thus ending a fine old English tradition.

The next 'top' is Hell's Gate, the lower entrance to the extensive hillfort. Built in the bronze age and rebuilt by iron age Celts, this was once the headquarters of the local tribe until the Romans ended it. It seems to have been a small town, fortified and with room to keep cattle and store grain; probably with a market. Just how it operated is little known compared with the Roman town which replaced it.

Hell's Gate, like its higher counterpart, Heaven's Gate, is a complicated structure. The walls were once faced with cut sandstone brought from the foot of the hill. There was a wall - ditch - wall construction, the gateway inturned with guardhouses each side. Above the walls was a stockade of timber. It would surely have been very difficult to enter the town without permission from those guarding it. How serious was the threat we do not know, but it must have taken a great deal of labour and organisation to construct such a fort. It has been suggested that hillforts were not really needed, and were merely a status symbol - but an expensive one.

It is unfortunate that there has been unnecessary wear of the hillfort gateways recently by horses, which have been ridden up the hill. Their riders far too often take them onto the walls, which has caused much damage. It is to be hoped that riders will try to understand that they are wearing away a very ancient monument; presumably not a thing they would do if they thought about it.

Dr. Stan Stanford, who was last to investigate the hillfort, has remarked on the style of the in-turned walls of the four gateways - there are two more on the south-west end. This method of building, he said, seems to have originated in the Danube valley, and there is a long trail of similar constructions from there to The Wrekin, the most northerly.

The tribe or nation concerned were called Cornovii and seem to have accepted Roman rule. A new capital not far away was built called Viroconium; it has been much more extensively dug by archaeologists and many reports have been written. The Saxons called this place Wroxeter; both names refer to The Wrekin.

There have only been two short 'digs' on The Wrekin; by Dr. Kathleen Kenyon before the second world war and by Dr. Stan Stanford before the TV transmitter was built. The enclosed map (page 61) shows the extent of the hillfort according to Dr. Kenyon. A few years ago a body was found in a peat bog near the Mersey. The man was described as a Druid, and may have been a human sacrifice. He belonged to the Cornovii, and lived in Roman times.

The map of the hillfort shown here is an adaptation of one drawn by Dr. Kenyon. It is a very large area and her investigation was interrupted by the second world war, so that there is a great deal of the fort which has not yet been seen since the first century AD. Without much further study there are no certain answers to the many questions which are asked.

It is believed that the fort was first built during the Bronze Age, at a time when the climate was deteriorating from its 'optimum'; an event which may have caused conflict over land as farming would have been made more difficult. It was extensively rebuilt in the early Iron Age and there is evidence of later repairs and rebuilding. This latter stage was done with much less skill and care than the earlier one, perhaps in a hurry. The dates suggest that it was at a time of expansion by Belgic tribes in the south-east.

It is interesting to try to imagine life on The Wrekin before the Romans changed things. Some of the men who lived here were warriors who went into battle with their bodies covered with woad and other colourings and nothing else unless tattoos are included. Their hair was limed and combed 'punk style'. They also made a dreadful noise according to accounts. They must have looked terrifying, perhaps hoping the enemy would run away. They were also probably drunk and high on mushroom juice. Yet, it is said, the Druids had such a hold over their people that they could walk between the battling lines with impunity.

Druids were highly trained priests who had learned tribal histories and rituals by heart after a very long apprenticeship. Their writing was in Ogam and they could converse using their hands, rather like people now who cannot speak. There were many holy places - pools, groves, trees and rocks. Some of what is believed to be their holy rocks are on The Wrekin - the Needle's Eye, the Cuckoo's Cup (or Raven's Bowls, the Bladder Stone and what some call the Calendar Stone).

The summit area is too bleak for most species of birds, with only the meadow pipit nesting, but watch for dotterel during migration periods. Sometimes hundreds of swift feed and the

Looking along the Wrekin - Stretton Fault.

The Needle's Eye.

occasional raven or buzzard can be seen.

Just over the top, on the south-west corner, is the Needle's Eye. It is a tradition that all true Salopians have climbed through from SW to NE. Girls must never look back. This may have been seen as the womb of the Earth Mother. It is not an easy climb (I have not been through since my 60th. birthday). It is a strange rock formation, apparently quite natural, with its vertical gully or chimney, a brief platform and an easier descent through a cleft. It is often said to be getting narrower - mainly by people who do not like to admit they are getting wider. A recent rock fall has made it impassable.

The Cuckoo's Cup always has water in a small bowl. The legend suggests that this is from a tear which was shed by one of two giants who were fighting for The Wrekin and was struck in the eye.

The Calendar Stone is just below it and here a finger of light comes through the rock at noon each equinox and alights on a flat stone for ten minutes, moving slowly over the surface. This only happens on these two days a year, and then only if the sun happens to be shining at the appropriate time. It has been discovered accidentally by two independent people and witnessed by others. Presumably the folk who lived on The Wrekin would have known. The equinoxes were most important times of change in the farming calendar. Perhaps there is another phenomena at dawn on the shortest day. But these things do not happen when there are too many clouds to see the sun. Anyone checking the truth of this story should note that midday comes ten minutes after noon at Greenwich as we are to the west by that amount. The Bladder Stone may refer to Baldur the god or to a boulder stone.

Apart from priests and warriors there were others, perhaps less glamorous, of the Cornovii. We have to remember that most of the population had to produce food; it is only very recently that agriculture has become so efficient that so many of us are relieved from this duty. There were also craftsmen and women; potters, weavers, metal workers, carpenters and so on, most of whom would have been also farmers. Most of the ordinary hand tools we now use had already been invented. Of course there would have been no farming on the hilltop; this took place in forest clearings where the best soil was found.

In Norman times there was a hermit who lived somewhere on The Wrekin in a cave. He was supposed to have been a holy man and the whole forest and hill were named Mount Gilbert for a time. There seems no trace of Gilbert's cave, though there were accounts of it being on view in the last century. This may forever be a secret of The Wrekin Forest. The Welsh name is Caer Gwrecon and in Saxon it was Wreoken. The origin is almost certainly pre-Celt, probably stone age. An old guide book claims Saxon origins, which cannot be true.

The top is marked by an Ordnance Survey trig. point, a small concrete pillar with a metal plate built in to support a theodolite in exactly the same place as last time. The height and position are established by triangulation, a very accurate method of surveying though much slower than modern laser technology. It may be surprising how many slightly different heights are given on various maps for the same hill; or perhaps the surprise is that they differ so little.

The trig. point is on some sort of mound which looks artificial. Perhaps it was for the beacons which were lit on the hill for special occasions. Lord Macaulay says in his poem 'The Armada' that, 'Streamed in crimson on the wind, The Wrekin's crest of light' He was describing the way in which the message of the Spanish Armada's sighting was spread through the country. The above lines rhyme with ...'Malvern's lonely height', though whether it is historically accurate is open to doubt. Other beacons were lit at the end of the war and to mark the Queen's silver jubilee.

To the north is a concrete slab which marks the spot where there was once an aircraft warning beacon. It was erected during the second world war after a crash resulting in the deaths of two Polish airmen, an instructor and his pupil. For a time this beacon was part of a network of lights which covered the country; it flashed red once a second. With the invention of radar and other electronic navigation equipment there was no need for it, but there was a great campaign to keep it going. Many local people had looked on this beacon with great affection; it was often the first sign of home to returning service men and women. For a while it was financed by public subscription although declared redundant by the air force, but the money ran out and it was demolished by volunteers from a local RAF unit. Presumably the remains went to the scrap yard.

Between the two 'tops' are several clear mounds which appear to be hut circles. Some are larger than the others. These have never been investigated and it would be interesting to know what an archaeologist makes of them. Unfortunately there is a shortage of competent persons and money to pay for their work. At the public inquiry into the planning permission for the TV station it was said that Dr. Stanford was one of a mere handful of archaeologists sufficiently experienced to carry out the investigation of the hillfort. Although it is an interesting subject for speculation one cannot but hope that there will be no dig unless it is supervised by a responsible expert, as otherwise irrevocable damage could be done.

The point where the beacon stood is not an artificial mound and bare rock projects over the steep tree lined slope. From here are the best views over north Shropshire and into Cheshire. During the war it was possible to see the barrage balloons at Liverpool. Most of the north is covered by glacial drift of clay or sand and gravel; now it is almost all farmland. Here and there

Hut circles.

SECRETS OF THE WREKIN FOREST

Severn, Wenlock Edge and the Clee Hills.

are small hills of sandstone, Grinshill and Hawkestone for example. These show the underlying Triassic rock, a desert sandstone, now called Lower Mottled or Bridgnorth sandstone, though it used to be called Bunter.

During the ice ages, if we had stood at this spot, we would have seen a bleak landscape of ice and snow; ice sheets covering all the land except for where we are, which would be bare rock. As the ice melted and tundra vegetation developed with extensive lakes and bogs we could have seen elk, deer and mammoth, perhaps pursued by wolves. Several milennia later the scene turns to broad leafed forest, rather like the oak-ash-birch forest we came through but much more extensive. Man had been here, however, all this time, and there would always have been some clearings with wood smoke rising from them.

Now we can pick out the creamery at Crudgington and the sugar factory at Allscott, both of which service the rich agricultural lands around. These two factories may be seen as alien in a rural landscape but the landscape is man made; fields, hedges and copses were planted and the milk and sugar beet produced here must be processed. Immediately below are conifer forests, stretching right up to the outcrop on which we stand, except for the left of our view, where the slope is very steep and bare of trees. Here we can easily pick out the slopes of the outer walls and ditches of the hillfort.

In the distance on the left are the foothills of Wales, with the Berwyns and a glimpse of Snowdon if it is exceptionally clear. Chirk castle has a seat in the garden called 'Wrekin View', though only the plume of smoke from Cronospan can be seen of Chirk. Rodney's Pillar on the Breidden Hills stands above Welshpool and next to Long Mountain. Looking along the line of The Wrekin to the Stretton Hills - Lawley, Caer Caradoc and the Ragleth, with their valley and the Long Mynd - it is easy to see the line of the Wrekin-Church Stretton fault. In the opposite direction Lilleshall Hill is on the same line.

Just to the north-north-east and below is the television transmitter. This is a blot on the landscape which many prefer not to notice, thrusting its intrusive concrete base and steel mast out of the side of the hill and obliterating part of the hillfort walls. It was opposed by many local people but permitted after a public inquiry. Some conservationists were confused into an 'either/or' argument against having it on the Stiperstones, which persuaded the Council for the Protection of Rural England to support the BBC's application. What was originally proposed, was a phallic symbol on the top.

To the north is the ancient village of Wrockwardine, another name with clear connections with The Wrekin; this may have been the Saxon headquarters of the area; it certainly was an important place still in Norman times as the chief settlement of the hundred. To the west, 'High the vanes of Shrewsbury gleam, Islanded in Severn stream,' as A.E.Houseman says in 'The Shropshire Lad'. Between Wellington and Shrewsbury the new much improved A5 has just been opened.

Looking southward, having crossed to the trig. point again for a better viewpoint the Wrekin/Stretton fault is still fairly obvious. To the left of the Stretton hills is the long line of Wenlock Edge, wooded and beautiful, stretching away from the Severn to Craven Arms. Below are farmlands and the river, which is more interesting when it is in flood, with its extensive flood-plain above the Ironbridge Gorge. The power station at Buildwas stands out in the same 'sore thumb' manner as the factories to the north. Yet the huge cooling towers and the slim tall chimney have a style of their own and there are some who would describe the building as having some charm.

Beyond Wenlock Edge are the Clee Hills - Brown Clee, the highest in Shropshire, with its masts and ancient coal mines and the more angular Titterstone, with its array of radar dishes pointing in the direction of what used to be the Soviet Union. All this is within the South Shropshire Area of Outstanding Natural Beauty, and we are at its most northerly point. It may be possible to glimpse the top of the Malvern Hills with the Brecon Beacons and the hills around Clun.

Further east are woodlands of The Wrekin Forest; the scars of quarrying for hardcore to build Telford new town are gradually mending on Maddock's Hill and The Ercall. Slowly nature is healing its wounds as the resurgent forest gradually rebuilds, beginning with the quicker growing colonising plants, followed by gorse, broom and birch, with oak and ash struggling along behind. Some of the new town estates still look extremely brash from the hilltop but the tree planting which has been part of the development is gradually having a mellowing effect. The tower blocks of Dudley stand starkly white on the skyline.

The Severn valley still shows the marks of the edge of the huge post-glacial lake which overflowed to gouge out the new valley of the river which became the Ironbridge Gorge. In the process it exposed Wenlock limestone and the coal measures, containing iron ore and fireclay which later became the basis for the industrial revolution. This geologically new area is still settling down and occasionally there are landslips.

Immediately below is the Cuckoo's Cup, which is always worth a visit, if only to see if there is still water in the tiny reservoir. To the right are the Bladder Stone and the Needle's Eye and below the Cuckoo's Cup is the Calendar Stone.

Looking over The Ercall one can see the sprawl of Telford, originally a collection of individually distinct towns and villages, some more affected by development than others.

Looking north-west from the top to Uppington and Aston.

Sunshine above the clouds - Caer Caradoc on the skyline.

Although it was the firm intention of the Development Corporation to unify the new town this was fortunately not possible and each settlement has managed to retain most of its unique character. There will be for some years scars where opencast coal working 'tidies up' parts of the coalfield which were previously mined by old fashioned methods. This replaces recolonised fields with eventually smooth contours, though it will take a much longer time for them to turn to natural soil.

A glance over towards Church Stretton will often be the best way to predict the weather over the next hour or so, as it usually comes from that direction. It is a fascinating exercise to watch the progress of a rain cloud coming towards The Wrekin; to see it raining over the fields and to watch if the wind is deflected north or south, or perhaps it will be high enough to sweep over the hill.

All this watching the landscape is, of course, only possible if the weather is right. There are many days in the year when viewing is quite impossible; when the hilltop is covered in mist or even thick fog, or when the countryside below is only dimly seen. Sometimes even at noon it is almost impossible to see where you are going. When there is a cloud on the top local people say The Wrekin has got its cap on. Usually there is a wind and old folks explain that 'Somebody left the gate open.'

A wonderful experience is when there is thick fog down below and the hilltop is clear, warm and sunny whilst below is cold and clammy. From the top can be seen just a few peaks like the Clees peeping above the fog, with no sign of life below except a puff of smoke from the power station.

Beside the trig. point the local Rotary Club has erected a toposcope in stone surmounted by a steel plate engraved with a diagram showing the directions and distances of places that can be seen on a good day. This is a great help to visitors and also provides a handy seat and background for photographs to prove their subjects made the ascent. It is the goal for an annual race by the boys and girls leaving Orleton Park School, who run from their school to here and back. The record time is around forty minutes, which seems very fast indeed.

Vegetation on the top, as for most of the upper ridge, is mainly grasses, heather, bilberry, low shrubs and a few stunted trees. From old photographs and picture postcards there appears to have been trees grown here in Victorian times, including pines. These were cut down during the Great War and have not been replaced. In any case the soil is as thin and poor as would be expected on the exposed hilltop. In many places there is only an inch or two at the most, the rest has been eroded and carried inexorably down the Severn. The lack of trees on the summit is a great advantage when viewing.

Much of the grass is a beautiful dark coloured fescue, thin and graceful and very comfortable to sit or lie on. There used to be a youth club whose members waited on the shortest Saturday night of the year to watch the dawn and spent the rest of the morning sleeping it off before going home. There is some grazing by rabbits but it is far from any place where there is enough soil to dig a burrow; and foxes keep the numbers down.

Occasionally one may see hang-gliders taking off into the wind, especially when it is from the east or north. Sometimes the wind is so strong that it is difficult to keep one's feet. This is also a popular venue for sponsored walks, which may involve dragging a car or a bed. Even in stormy conditions there are families who climb the hill at midnight on New Year's Eve to drink the toast to 'All Friends Around The Wrekin'. Others bring their Christmas lunch and eat it on the top. Some years ago the County Education Secretary was in the habit of bringing his most difficult problems up here for solution.

When there are local events, such as Shrewsbury Flower Show, there are vehicles supplementing the TV mast as transmitting posts. The army too, when involved in an exercise, use a truck as a mobile radio station. Apart from these there should be no vehicles.

A few years ago there was an extensive fire on the south side which destroyed vegetation from below the Cuckoo's Cup to beyond the Needle's Eye. This necessitated a fire engine and water was pumped from the reservoir at the foot. Although there were fears that the whole forest would be gutted this fire turned out to be less dangerous than it could have been, though it would hardly have been popular with the firemen, some of whom had to stay on the top all night. The fire was started by children. There seems to be a great temptation for fires to be lit in various parts of the forest and there have been several out of control over the years. At the two Scout camps vandals have set fire to buildings, though the Scouts and Guides are better trained and more thoughtful; their own fires are properly controlled.

Because The Wrekin is such a wonderful place it is tempting to encourage tourism, to persuade more and more people to enjoy it. Unfortunately we tend to destroy those places we love and the numbers are already too many. Grass grows by inches, but is killed by feet. The number of feet on this hill is already as high as it will take; erosion is in danger of getting out of hand. Those of us who care for the world's wild places, of which this is surely one, small as it is, must be constantly vigilant. It is vulnerable to exploitation, and carelessness too, so we must exhort our friends to love it and care for its unique beauty.

Trig. point and toposcope.

Chapter Three

SURROUNDING WOODLANDS – ALL ROUND THE WREKIN

F ROM NEAR the eastern end of the Wrekin Course, which is an 'enclosure' road built across the old Wrekin Liberty, is a convenient entrance to the woods surrounding The Wrekin. There is room to park a few cars, which accounts for the normally filthy litter-strewn look of the place. It seems that once people are a hundred yards or so from their cars they become caring, sensible and civilised but where there is a car park and in this case it is only by implied permission of a long suffering landowner - litter must be strewn.

There used to be an iron gate here but that is long gone. The track is made up with stone, a pleasant walk. On our left trees are mostly young and small, natural regeneration which will grow into forest given time. There are many birch trees and a large part of the area is covered in bracken. Most of this wood is well drained, the lower slopes of the hill. There are occasional older trees including holly, rowan and hawthorn.

There are informal paths to the Forest Glen, around the top corner of the field and short cuts to the upper track leading to Wrekin Cottage. We take the 'official' track and come to an interesting spring on the left hand side under a holly and overlooked by an old yew. This is said to be unusually pure water, gushing from the fault line between the sandstone and the Wrekin volcanic series. The water crosses the track and becomes a little stream - the south Shropshire word is a prill.

There are hollies and some yews, but most of the trees are birch, rowan, sycamore, ash or hazel. All appear naturally grown, though there is some coppicing. We come now to a wide junction, where the track turns left up the hill; almost straight for some way. On our left, set back from the road, are the remains of the 'Burnt Cottage'. Most local people know this as the burnt cottage area, even those who have never found the vaulted brick arches, the remains of the cellars; these are almost the only sign of there having been a house here. Other signs are a few garden escapes and ornamental trees and shrubs.

Here was once the Lower Wrekin Cottage (as distinct from the one higher). It is said that there were two old ladies living here when the fire destroyed the house. Years ago there were

Remains of the Burnt Cottage.

The beech avenue.

more bricks but these have disappeared. An old picture, which I have been unable to trace, showed a large cottage. It is said to have been used as a hunting lodge in ancient times and to have gradually declined.

The track going upwards is usually called the burnt cottage path. For its first, straight, section it makes an excellent sledge run if the snow is right and the trees at the bottom are avoided. Another hazard to sledges is a rock to the west of the track, which, if hit at speed, catapults the sledge and rider into a ditch. At the first corner it may be rather muddy. From this point there is a magnificent avenue of ancient beech trees, some of which may be fallen. This avenue continues to the cottage, backed by mature oaks, ash and the occasional sycamore or birch on both sides. It is an excellent walk, rising gently, with the ground sloping steeply on both sides, up and down.

At the first bend there is a small steep path leading up to the right which joins the 'Sentry's Path' on a ridge and continues left to the top ridge; it is a short cut for the agile. The sentries referred to were from the rifle range - of which later - who used to have instructions to run up to the ridge to warn the public of the danger of straying too near to the firing line. This is no longer the practice and notices are relied on. There is a warning notice on the bend and the Ordnance Survey map shows the extent of the danger area, though occasional ricochets are heard overhead on the ridge.

About half way between first corner and cottage there is a track leading to the right which is not a public footpath but known as the charcoal burners' track. It is not now used and may be very difficult to find, especially when the leaves are on the trees. It is not advisable to investigate it if there is firing on the rifle range, as it traverses above the targets and a ricochet or a wild shot might easily cause casualties. There is no warning on this corner, perhaps because there is no obvious path.

Charcoal burning was an important industry all over this forest for many centuries until early this century for until 1709 it was the common fuel for iron working. Even this century there was coppicing for charcoal by Grooms of Wellington. In the 1930s Alf Wilks was the foreman of the timbermen who cut wood for the kiln in Wellington. Until this was built the charcoal was burnt in large mounds in the woods, with turf being used to control the air supply and thus the burning. This part of the forest has not been used for timber since the 1930s, and so it is a haven for wildlife.

If you have a copy of the Wrekin Orienteers' map you will find small platforms marked. Scratch the ground here with a stick and you will almost certainly find that charcoal has been made on this spot. Many of the trees have been planted or coppiced for charcoal or felled for timber production. It is only quite recently that this part of the forest has been left for wildlife.

Conservationists should be grateful that the Orleton estate, who own the land, have left it alone.

Early conservationists included Saxon and Norman kings, for this was a Royal Forest until the late middle ages. Their aim, through forest laws, was to conserve the deer and boar for their hunting and there were strict penalties for any peasants who offended. There were, however, rights which peasants had too, such as the collection of firewood and some grazing of pigs. Timber for building was allowed with permission and the forest was a sort of DIY shop. Just before the 'Glorious Revolution' one owner of this forest was caught with a houseful of weapons and gunpowder and forced to sell all the timber in his woodlands to pay his fine. He was very fortunate to be so lightly treated, but the effect on the forest must have been devastating.

At the time of writing there are several landowners and only two small parts of the whole forest - the northern slopes of The Ercall and of the Limekiln Woods - are owned by public bodies; Shropshire County and Wrekin District Councils. The only rights we have as members of the public on the rest of the forest are to walk and in places ride horses; and that only on designated footpaths. Otherwise we are trespassing.

Soon we come to the cottage, which we have seen on the last walk. We pass this house lamenting, perhaps that it is no longer providing refreshments, walk down the track and turn right below onto the perimeter track, on the south side of the hill, heading south-west. The remains of the pigstyes are on our left, with some interesting mosses. The track is broad and pleasant and we cross a small stream, with farmland on our left, mostly grazing sheep, cattle and horses. On the geological map the fields appear to coincide with Wrekin Quartzite, a Cambrian rock, whilst the woods on our right are on the ancient Wrekin volcanics.

Another stream crosses the path and there is woodland on the left as well as right. There is a path to the left along the edge of the wood, across the fields and the farm lane into Wenlock's Wood. This is thick deciduous woodland, not coppiced for fifty years or so and used for raising and shooting pheasants. Extreme care should be taken, even on the public path, during shoots. The path comes out eventually on the Willowmoor Bank. This area will be considered in chapter five.

To return to the perimeter track; there are soon larches on the right as the ownership changes to Raby estates, where the policy is to grow timber, mainly conifers, commercially. A path rises steeply to the Cuckoo's Cup through a plantation of sycamore. There is now a fork, straight on to the Little Hill and left to the Scout Camp. A little further down is another fork, left to the camp and right to Neves Castle. Gibbons Coppice, on the left of the Scout Trail, is

The Cuckoo's Cup from a camp site in Gibbons Coppice.

Second Wellington Troop Scout Hut.

mainly deciduous. There are buildings on both sides connected with the camp; a very ancient looking hut belonging to the 2nd Wellington Troop, a climbing tower, a swimming pool and a chapel on the left and latrine and ablution blocks on the right. Unfortunately the scouts have been attacked by arsonist vandals and their storm hut destroyed. Here and there are clearings for tents and there is a camp fire circle. This camp has been in constant use since at least the 1930s. Some of us used to 'run away from home' to here every fine weekend. It becomes increasingly sophisticated but presumably is still fun.

A recent development in Gibbons Coppice has been the clearing of several broad tracks, wide enough for fire breaks or walks. Some of the ash and elm trees were felled in the 1930s for aircraft manufacture. Most of the undergrowth here shows it to be ancient forest, and is semi-natural. There is a great variety of vegetation types, quite a contrast between damp and dry areas.

There are various conifer plantations from here to the Little Hill and Neves Castle. The rides make pleasant walks but are not public rights of way. A forester working in another part of Shropshire, when answering criticisms of conifer plantations, replied with the question, 'If these plantations are so dreadfully ugly why is it that so many people walk in them so often?'

The types of conifers vary with the plantation; there are larches, spruce, fir, occasional cedars, cypresses and pines. Also planted are beech, sycamore, oak and ash, and many unplanted holly, yew, rowan, and other indigenous varieties. For some years it has been policy to do 'dapple shade planting' - to leave deciduous trees standing when faster growing conifers are cropped and to re-plant conifers under their shade. There has been a more recent trend to plant small oak among the young conifers to grow on with them and make the final crop oak after the conifers have been harvested.

There has often been an outcry from 'the townies' when an area is cropped. What else were they planted for? No-one expects a farmer to leave his wheat crop in the ground! Not only does this type of land-use provide timber for its many uses but it also is the livelihood of the men who work the land. It would be unreasonable for the writer of this book - which is made of timber - to try to justify the ban on timber production which some would advocate; and conifers grow far faster than hardwoods.

It is also true that the Little Hill used to be called Primrose Hill, and the conifers have put paid to the primroses and a good many other wild flowers which used to flourish there and in other parts of this woodland. The sometimes dense tree cover has led to a lack of undergrowth and the needles have turned the soil acid. Within some of the densest plantations there is almost none of the natural vegetation which was once there except along the rides, though

Beech, sycamore and yew - variety within the conifer plantations.

these reveal some of the ancient trees, shrubs and undergrowth, the bird life and other wild animals which once were more widespread.

One could say the same for many suburban gardens. In fact most of what is generally called 'gardening' consists of killing off the natural vegetation ('weeds') to encourage exotic and man made species.

In spring the larches have such a wonderful scent that it is well worth while to walk through a larch plantation for this alone. Yet even within this commercial forest one can still come across the scent of a bluebell wood.

Back to the upper fork in the track. If we take the level track it follows the contours towards the Little Hill. Unless the trees have grown too tall there are fine views from here to the south. About half way between the fork and the Little Hill on the right is a grove of yew trees which deserves investigation.

The age of these trees is a cause for wonderment, as they spread from a huge old trunk, 18 ft. 6 ins. in circumference. 1,000 years? Maybe more. Immediately above is the Needle's Eye, and yew trees are of ancient religious significance. It has recently become fashionable to believe that far from being planted in Christian churchyards the opposite is often true that the church was built in a yew grove. So I am suggesting that this yew grove is well over 2,000 years old. Perhaps some day we shall know, though I must hope that is not because someone has cut them down to count the rings!

There is an interesting account of the latest thinking on ancient yew trees in Andrew Morton's book 'Trees of Shropshire.' It is unfortunate that he does not include this tree (or grove of trees). If he, and others, are right yews grow quite quickly to begin with (there is a vigorous young yew in my garden) and later their growth slows until after a thousand years or so the trunk begins to rot and becomes hollow inside. After another few hundred years it regenerates and grows a new trunk. Here there are many new trunks grown on the outside, at least 13' 6" from the centre. The soil here is only a very few inches thick, which would slow growth. Yews are connected very strongly with ancient religions, and the position of this tree (or trees) below the Needle's Eye, an ancient religious site, gives extra credence to the possibility of its being of great age. This could, just possibly, be more ancient than any other yew - or rather it could be the oldest tree in the world! We may have to think of it as being pre-Celt, say 2,500 years or more. Allen Meredith, who has investigated many such trees should see this one.

A little further there appears to be an ancient house site on the left. I am told that it was called the 'windy cocarth' (coke hearth or charcoal burning site). It is just at the point where

The 'Log Slide', Little Hill.

the downward slope on the left of the track levels off. We now arrive at the saddle between The Wrekin and the Little Hill, and here is a cross-roads. The right hand track goes steeply up the ridge towards the Needle's Eye. The views to the south from here are magnificent, but to the north the trees are too high to allow a sight of the Shropshire Plain until nearly the top.

Several outcrops give convenient seats for admiring the scenery and an excuse to pause. This is another excellent sledge or ski run when the snow is right but is not for the faint hearted or inexperienced as it is steep. At the top are two inturned gateways - the 'back gates' - which complement Heaven and Hell Gates. One is each side the Needle's Eye, which can be approached from this direction. The top of the ancient yew tree can be seen from here. There are also daffodils!

To return to the crossroads on the saddle; the track northwards leads down to join the perimeter track on that side. We shall take the continuation of the ridge track, descend a little and climb gently to the summit of the Little Hill. Here are several small circular mounds with pine trees planted in them which used to be called the Druids' Circles. Unfortunately these pines appear near the end of their lives and many of them have died. One is called the Magic Tree - but that is a family tradition which cannot be told. Some secrets should remain.

There is usually a tree trunk to sit on at this little summit and the view is worth taking the time to see, preferably with a good map. In the centre of the view is Caer Caradoc, reminding us that the Church Stretton fault is also The Wrekin fault. Between is a broad vista of farmland and woods, villages and farms. It is only possible to enjoy this scene until the trees grow high enough to hide it, for they are planted right up to the top, and when they mature they will hide the view.

Right ahead the track is straight and steep; it is often called the log slide. It would be a good test for the brakes of a mountain bike. Here is an interesting place to look at the erosion caused by normal weather on the hillside, and on each side one can see the effect of the vegetation in curbing this erosion. The rocks outcropping are well described by Peter Toghill in his 'Geology of Shropshire'. These are the preCambrian gneisses, the oldest rocks on The Wrekin.

At the bottom of this slope are many wide tracks between plantations of conifers interspersed with indigenous species including hornbeam. Most of these are not public rights of way. The first crossroads goes right to join the perimeter track and left to a wooden hut hidden in trees. The second crossroads leads right to a well used gate onto the road and left through the woods to a lower perimeter track. This track has below its surface the gas pipe carrying North Sea gas to the Wellington distribution centre.

Walking along the track straight ahead we slope steadily downwards, and at times it is rather

May Plantation.

muddy. Although we are in conifer plantations they are by no means as boring as that may suggest. The trees are of different varieties and there are variations in the slopes on each side worth investigating. Here and there are mounds and pits, some clearly man made are saw pits. Apparently there was a framework above the pit holding the log, with one man above and one below, operating a crosscut saw. The man in the pit must have looked forward to becoming the man on top! Some of the ridges look like hedgerows without the hedges; this was agricultural land not so long ago. There are also natural slope variations and many odd trees and bushes which have been left when the conifers were planted. There are enough puzzles of this kind to make it an interesting walk.

If we carry straight on our track ends at Neves Castle, an intriguing place. There is a farmhouse on what appears to be an artificial mound, suggesting a mott. There is little else to see and I have seen little documentation, apart from a note in 'Castles of Shropshire' by Michael Jackson, who mentions it in his appendix without any explanation. Perhaps it was a Knaves' castle, a place of robbers, of outlaws who hid in the forest? There are many romantic possibilities to be dreamed of.

At the edge of the forest, from here round to the rifle range, is a fascinating avenue of lime trees. They must be at least sixty years old and have grown tall and have the common growth of twigs around the trunk from the ground to about six feet high. Presumably planted as rides, the space between the trees seems not to be much used recently and in places is almost impassable. The avenue extends along the forest edge from Spout Lane, through Neves Castle, across the entrance to White Cottage Plantation (suggesting that it predates this) and along the north-west to the field containing the rifle range. It is a fine avenue and an interesting anomaly.

From Rushton Lane runs a track along the north-west side of The Wrekin. It begins by a house advertising its guard dogs and passes through newly planted conifers with oak interplanted, across several forest tracks, some with beech trees, and past the entrance to the Seascout camp. There is a long connection between Walsall, Seascouts and The Wrekin, which would be difficult to connect logically with the sea. But the camp is tidy and well maintained, with an ingenious water supply and some wooden huts. Again there has been vandalism and arson attacks, surprising as so few people go this way, and the scouts can hardly be causing a nuisance to anyone. But perhaps I am trying to make sense of senselessness. Here are ancient yews and hollies, and the ground around has been carefully drained. There are also pub signs - another anomaly.

From the northern perimeter leads a track towards White Cottage Plantation, a long strip of woodland stretching to the north-west. It appears to be new in the sense that it has been

Near White Cottage Plantation.

farmland which has been added to the woods, rather than a continuous part of the forest. The only public footpath into it reinforces this idea of separateness, as it simply connects the Wrekin Course with the Rushton road and has no connection with the other forest paths. There are few trees in this wood that are more than about fifty years old. Some are hardwoods, so the undergrowth is interesting. The lime avenue continues along the edge of the forest but seems to ignore this wood.

From here towards the Rifle Range the track runs roughly along the boundary between the Triassic sandstone and the much more ancient Wrekin volcanic series. One of the secrets which The Wrekin is keeping from me, if not from others, is the source of the sandstone which was used to face the hillfort walls. Dr. Kathleen Kenyon found in her excavations just before the second world war that at least parts of the huge walls around the camp had been constructed with ashlar, which was what is nowadays called LMS or lower mottled sandstone.

The amount of work involved in cutting and carting enough stone to build the walls must have been very great. The puzzle is not so much how this was done but where are the quarries from which the stone was taken. There are a few small places which could possibly have been used, but there must have been many more or one much larger quarry, which simply does not want to be found. The other question is why? Why would the people living at the top of the hill go to the trouble of heaving all this stone from the bottom of the hill to the top, just to ensure that their walls looked smarter? And who did the work? Slaves, presumably.

Halfway to the rifle range is a fork; the left hand is the right of way, whilst the right hand track leads upwards in a series of zig-zags towards the ridge without actually arriving there. These tracks are for forestry use, intended to facilitate the movement of timber, not for walkers.

Meanwhile the perimeter track is a very pleasant walk, gently undulating and with occasional views out over the woods to the north. Here are some sweet chestnut trees along the track. Ridges go across, with small valleys containing hillwash; stones and earth washed down from the hill as the ice sheets melted and frost and melt hastened the disintegration of the rocks. Looking up one can see that a part of the hill's flank is bare of trees, though there are bushes of hawthorn, hazel, rowan and elder. Here I have caught the acrid smell of a fox marking his territory with urine - exciting, if unpleasant!

Within the plantations on the left are, so it is believed, the Soldiers' Graves and the Battlebank. It is said that here were found the remains of men killed in battle. Some have assumed that this was a battle for The Wrekin with the Romans. If so it would be difficult to explain why the Celts would have come out from their fortifications to fight their enemy on the lower slopes, rather than sitting tight and using the advantages of the steep hillside and the wall and ditch defences. We are told that there was probably no battle with the Romans, and that the Viriconii, Cornovii or whatever they called themselves at the time accepted Roman rule. There certainly does not seem to be any other evidence or record of a fight, and it is assumed that the Romans were seen as preferable to the Belgic Celts of the south-east who were in an expansionist phase just before the Roman invasion.

This, if true, does not rule out a battle; after all the Romans were not the only warlike people to come this way, surely. It would be interesting to know the truth of the matter. There are many places like this on The Wrekin which would repay investigation - but only a proper inquiry by archaeologists suitably qualified, not just a hasty dig by treasure hunters who would simply destroy evidence without understanding what they were doing. Part of the story which is particularly intriguing is that the human remains were of exceptionally tall men. It makes one think of warrior races such as the Batutsi, who were able to impose their will on smaller peoples, and to 'farm with the spear', meaning to use their spears to ensure that others did the farming for them.

Further on we come to the Wrekin Rifle Range. This has been in operation for a good many years, and is a considerable problem in that it extends across the public right of way. In fact the targets are on the track. So I do not recommend using the path if there is firing! At times the butts across the Wrekin Course are used to get a longer distance and this means the road too has to be closed.The range has been in use since at least the Great War, and is mainly used now by Territorials and Cadets. During WW2 the Home Guard made extensive use of it.

There was a campaign against the continued use of this range during the 1970s. A petition was signed, there was press coverage - local and national - and TV news agencies were interested. The result was that the Minister announced a decision that use would be discontinued and the range transferred elsewhere. Twenty years later nothing has changed.

It has been pointed out that so far as wild life is concerned the range may actually be an advantage. Surprisingly this may well be true, as the very danger to humans keeps us away at times, and we are the only real inhibitors of animal life, particularly birds and foxes. The range is not now greatly used; most days it is free.

From here it is only a short walk to the Burnt Cottage, past one of the quarries which may have supplied sandstone for the hillfort walls. We have circumnavigated The Wrekin, without leaving the forest.

Woods near Burnt Cottage.

Chapter Four

THE ERCALL, LAWRENCE'S HILL AND FOREST GLEN

Note - Ercall is pronounced Arcall, as are the villages of High Ercall and Childs Ercall. It is presumably an ancient name, like The Wrekin, of Celtic or more likely pre-Celtic origin.

THE M54 motorway drove a deep cutting through the volcanic rocks of The Ercall, destroying the forest as it went. This left a small piece of woodland to the north in the grounds of The Russets, the last house on Ercall Lane. The wood is species rich, containing several springs along the fault line which divides a dry slope to the south from a very wet lower section in the north. The dry part has the same oak/birch trees as the rest of the upper Ercall, with some heather and bilberry, but below the fault are wetland species, including horse-tails, survivors from the Carboniferous age.

This small wood has been fenced off, and although the footpaths around it have been preserved it is virtually a private garden, though a nature reserve, full of squirrels and birds. The springs give rise to a stream which joins another watercourse coming down from The Ercall under the M54. The stream from The Ercall is mostly run-off and is greatly affected by the weather, whereas the springs are from underground and never seem to vary, even in the driest times. The confluence is close to the path to Christine Avenue, where there is a small bridge; in a drought it will be seen that only the spring water is flowing, whilst after heavy rain the runoff stream dominates.

The largest of the springs lies under an ancient hollybush and is marked as a well on the Ordnance Survey Pathfinder. Its water appears extremely pure and it is exactly on the geological fault. A well used path went past here until the wood was fenced off. Since that time there have been few intrusions, which has been better for the wildlife than for the many local people who used to walk here. Before the M54 was built this area was part of the Wrekin Site of Special Scientific Interest, but for reasons, which may be understood by the NCC (now English Nature) but certainly not by me, it was deleted.

Russets Wood is an interesting illustration of the effects of human contacts on the natural world. Most of us would like to have our cake and eat it, abundant nature with public access,

M54 cutting through The Ercall.

Fungi on birch at The Ercall.

but in fact the two are not mutually compatible. When it was open to everyone some birds were frightened off and plants were trampled. Now that we, the public, are excluded it is far more accessible to nature; there is no litter and the only sounds, from inside at least, are bird songs.

One path leads along above the motorway cutting from Ercall Lane, down steeply to the stream and along below an embankment to Golf Links Lane near the point where there is an underpass. At the stream another path from Christine Avenue joins it. This latter passes alongside the stream which is deeply entrenched at first and then almost at the same level, so that the path is supported on a wooden walkway. It crosses the spring-stream near the confluence on a small bridge and between two houses arrives at Christine Avenue.

There are clumps of bluebells, glowing sweet-scented blue in the spring and a wealth of other delightful wild flowers in their seasons. Many of the trees have nesting boxes and there is a great variety of birdlife. But this is semi-natural woodland; there are changes of slope there have been human intrusions, at one place suggesting an ancient road-way and at another a quarry. Some of the trees have been coppiced and others planted. There are garden escapes from the houses which surround on three sides. There is no no trace of the rolls of barbed wire put up by the Home Guard to protect Wellington from the infiltration of German paratroops during the second world war.

When the M54 was being constructed a deep cutting was excavated in The Ercall. The Precambrian volcanic rock, a soft ash, which was extracted was unsuitable for hardcore, so it was removed but the contractors brought it back again and used it just the same. Perhaps that is one reason why it has been called the worst built motorway in the world and has been constantly under repair since it was opened.

This yellowish-grey rock is soft and consists of very fine ashes from some ancient volcano, though it would be a mistake to suppose that it was extruded from The Ercall, as this was before the massive earth movements which gave it its present shape. According to current geological thinking the volcanic eruption took place when our part of the earth was as far south as Australia. The cutting is well covered in gorse and broom and the inevitable silver birches have colonised the newly bare rock. Earlier colonisation by fireweed (rosebay willow herb) is being edged out by stronger growth.

Over the motorway bridge on Ercall Lane the hill up to its ridge is owned by Shropshire County Council, who have built a small car park in one of the old quarries. There is a dispute as to the use of these quarries; Andrew Jenkinson has suggested that they were primarily for china-clay, which was formed by the disintegration of the granophyre (as in Cornwall granite), and used for the local china works. Others are sure that the only use was for making roads and paths. The distinctive pink colouring of the granophyre, here called Ercallite, can certainly be seen in many old roads. Evidence suggests that Telford used it for his Holyhead Road as far away as St. Georges, and some believe that the Romans had used the same top dressing for their Watling Street, the same road, 1,600 years earlier. Certainly many local paths at Dothill, Apley or Wellington cemetery have this unusual pink stone.

Along the side of Ercall Lane, for most of its way by the woodland, are several small old quarries. According to the Ordnance Survey map there was a Roman palstave found here in Victorian times. One cannot but wonder whether this had anything to do with the use of granophyre as a top dressing for the Watling Street, and why a Roman was careless enough to lose it.

Many thousands of tons of Ercallite must have been taken from here by waggons, which at one time stopped at the weighbridge near a cottage down the road. This is a very popular walking area; so popular in fact that near the car park the vegetation has been worn away. There are many small paths, some of which have been made up with steps by the Council's Ranger, Ron Felton, and volunteers. One particularly delightful path is about half way up the side of the hill, traversing towards The Wrekin. From the western end there is a long flight of steps up to the ridge, arriving at an outcrop of quartzite, called by some Carreg Hen.

The ridge makes a very popular walk. There are many twisted old oaks, bent by the force of the wind. We know a group of these as the Climbing Trees because it is almost impossible to get children to walk past - they really must be climbed, and are actually very easy. One always had a drop of water in a broken branch and is called the Pani (water) tree and another, which had been blown over many years ago and leans against a neighbouring tree as the Lazy Oak. There is a small deviation from the path where there is a fine view over the woods and the golf links to Maddocks Hill and many parts of Telford called Lookout Point. From here you can also see the tower blocks at Dudley - if you really want to. I am constantly apologising for the fact that the undergrowth has been destroyed here by far too many feet; it is my fault because I have brought too many children here over the years. They enjoyed it but the effect on the environment has been a disaster which continues as they bring their children and even grandchildren.

The top of The Ercall has the remains of a small hillfort, some of which has been destroyed by quarrying. A visit to the west end of the top shows the huge quarries which are the price the environment has paid for the building of Telford New Town. The rock extracted was Wrekin quartzite for use as hardcore. We will take a closer look at these quarries later; in the meantime, this is the view (apart from the quarries) which appears in the 1948 Geological Survey's

'Climbing Trees', The Ercall.

'Lookout Point', Golf Course and Limekiln Wood.

handbook on the Welsh Borderland. It is a good place to stop for a while, for there is a lot to be seen.

Between the Ercall ridge and the golf course to the south is a woodland very rich in variety. Nearly all of it is ancient semi-natural forest, used and managed for many centuries, with the undergrowth which would be expected, including groves of bluebells, the finest flower of natural England. In several places along this path the bluebells shimmer brightly in the dappled spring sunshine bringing a magical atmosphere.

South of the ridge is generally dry wood, mainly oak and birch on shallow soils with quartzite or Ercallite an inch or so down. Here grow fungi in the autumn of many kinds including the 'beefsteak' varieties on the trees and the brilliant red fly agaric. As in most of the forest these trees were last coppiced in the 1930s, since when they have been left alone. The result is that some of them have been blown down in high winds, others are rotting and providing food for insects, who are in turn eaten by birds, and new growth is taking place.

The wetter lands below the hill and between it and the golf course have a different collection of plants, including the wild garlic and other wetland species. Here are many hollies which like the wet soil; there must be several hundred small holly trees and bushes. A stream flows through these 'wet, wild woods' as Kipling would say, rising from a muddy spring in the west and running westwards. This eventually goes under the motorway and is the one which crosses Christine Avenue.

In places this woodland is very damp and has less visitors. There is a public path along the base of the hill which becomes braided in wetter places as walkers try to keep out of the mud. Along this path was once the caravan of a well known local character called Lil. She lived here with her husband and a very large number of assorted dogs and cats for many years. It took many visits from officials and at least two court orders to persuade her to leave the woods and be rehoused in a council house.

Between this wood and Golf Links Lane (which is much older than any golf links and used to be known as Hollybush Lane) is a small meadow. Here is a profusion of the kind of wild flowers which always used to grace meadows before the introduction of modern fertilisers, weedkillers, planted grasses and modern management. There are few of these magical places left now; it is grazed only by a few horses from the riding school and is otherwise cut for a little hay and left to its own devices. This meadow is a little gem of its kind, a relic of the many small clearings which were once in the great Wrekin Forest; it deserves to be protected for there is almost no equivalent place. To retain its wildflowers it needs to be managed grazed and cut for hay - otherwise it will revert to forest.

Ochre Spring, Ercall Quarries.

Opposite the Buckatree Hall Hotel is the entrance to a large collection of mainly recent quarries. They have bitten huge chunks out of The Ercall and Lawrence hills in the course of extracting hardcore to make the roads and buildings of the new town. Nearly all the rock extracted has been Cambrian quartzite. The resultant landscape is a geologist's delight, for many interesting features have been exposed; it is also a conservationist's nightmare, with all the natural vegetation and soils stripped off, leaving bare rock.

There have been several attempts to get planning permission for development in these quarries, including a mini-Alton Towers with rides and plastic dinosaurs and a holiday camp of chalets. There has also been talk of a caravan park. Two schools of thought are almost diametrically opposed; one is that this is derelict land which should be constructively used by the public, the other maintains that we have already lost far too much of our natural heritage and that the forest should be allowed to regenerate and heal the scars which have been inflicted on it. For six or seven years the battle has raged and at the moment the conservationist view has prevailed, though there is never an end to this argument and the final outcome has yet to be decided.

The regeneration of the forest is a truly fascinating study. Here, with a very little help at the end of the quarrying, the forest is forcing a comeback, recolonising bare rock and rubble at a most astonishing rate. Some of the older slopes on The Ercall have quite large silver birches growing in high crevices and on tiny ledges. First frost, rain and bacteria have broken down the rock into soil; this has been colonised by rosebay, dandelion and other windblown seeds, which in their turn have improved the soil and been ousted by hardier growths, especially gorse, heather, bilberry, grasses and birch, ash and rowan trees. Humus from the plant leaves and bird droppings also contribute to the development of soil.

Last year, 1991, subsoil from a building development was dumped on a part of the quarry which was regenerating rather well. The initial effect was to destroy all the new growth but there are signs that nature will win again if it is left alone. Travellers caused another environmental disaster at the end of 1991, burning timber for fires and destroying vegetation.

There is a stream flowing through the quarries from the golf course to the south through a fine rich wetland to empty into the small lake at Buckatree Hall Hotel which was once the source of water for Wellington. The lake was made as a reservoir, though it has not been used for this purpose for almost a century. Within the quarry there is a small spring from which comes 'ochre water', a dark red-brown rusty colour, which joins the stream. The iron oxide from this spring is one of the attractions to geologists.

Lawrence's Hill quarry from the top of the Ercall.

Peter Toghill describes the Cambrian rocks as being laid down when England was around 65 degrees south of the equator and Scotland was about 6,000 km. to the north, across the Iapetus Ocean. He informs us that the Wrekin quartzite is really a sandstone rather than a quartzite, as it was not metamorphosed by intense heat and pressure as a true quartzite has been. Geologists are particularly interested in ripple marks in this rock, showing where there was once a seashore and also its junctions with the earlier volcanic series and the intrusive Ercallite. All these are well exposed on the quarry faces, and in places there is extensive 'geological erosion' meaning erosion of rock by geologists. The quarries are one of the reasons that The Wrekin Hills are designated as a Site of Special Scientific Interest.

The sandstone called Wrekin Quartzite is particularly well exposed, showing its grain and the angle of the strata. At its base is a conglomerate containing pebbles of locally derived rhyolites, tuffs and granophyre. These pebbles are often altered to a green colour caused by chlorite, derived from iron-bearing minerals and bright yellow from limonite (iron oxide). There are few fossils in the sandstone apart from trace-fossils of worm borings.

The Ercall granophyre is a fine grained granitic rock which was intruded into the Uriconian volcanic series and both are overlain unconformably by the quartzite. Ercallite is a pretty pink colour with a fine grain; under the microscope it shows a beautiful intergrowth of quartz and feldspar crystals resembling hieroglyphics. Ercallite is dated at 560 or 533 million years ago. The quarries are often visited by parties of students from various universities and colleges and a local comprehensive school with a particularly active geological department.

Lawrence's Hill (or St. Lawrence's Hill) has been badly bitten by quarrying but what remains of the hill is a pleasant place. It is mainly of coarse ash, now that the quartzite has gone; the ash contains volcanic bombs and intrusive dykes of dolerite on the Forest Glen side. On the top and sides are thin dry soils with planted conifers, mainly larch with some pines, and thick bracken where the soil is a little deeper, with heather and bilberry. On the side next to the Forest Glen are outcrops of hard black dolerite, which appears to have been extracted in quarries which allowed the Pavilion and its car park to have been built. These provide difficult and dangerous climbs from which young climbers have to be rescued by the fire brigade. Some have left their names in graffiti on the rock face.

On the south side of Lawrence's Hill is a small valley which contains the Dairy Pit or Davy Pit. Here, according to legend, is a 'marmid' or mermaid who attracts unwary travellers to join her in the water. The pit is a circular pool surrounded by five artificial mounds, assumed to be bronze age tumuli or burial mounds. Recently it has been said that this site is not the 3,000 or more year old burial ground previously supposed, but a much more recent trial mining dig.

May I suggest that before deciding which is true you go there at night, alone, and stand silently. If the hair on the back of your neck tells you of the presence of the ancient dead, then you will know, as I know, that this place is unique. There are many tumuli of this age but I know of no other site where they surround a pool.

The Dairy Pit is another of the truly magical places around The Wrekin and no-one I have met has failed to be impressed by the aura of ancient sanctity which it has. There must be a spring under the pool, for it is never empty and trickles away to the west. An avenue of planted conifers joins it to the Forest Glen road but there are not many visitors as it is difficult to find. The water is full of vegetation and always green except when frozen solid and covered by snow. Yet the Dairy Pit has many moods; it changes in colour with the seasons and the sky. At times it is covered in a light mist or it may be hoar frost or fallen leaves or the first spurts of spring green. On a fine day there is light dappled sunshine but in the light of the moon, when dark clouds cross the sky, and there is no sound but the wind, then it is at its most eerie.

South of here is a low ridge of Comley sandstone and Shineton shales; in fact there are two such ridges between The Ercall-Lawrence ridge and the golf course, divided by the stream which flows through the quarries. One ridge has a fox earth and the other two very ancient yew trees. Both ridges are ancient forest, cut, planted and coppiced over the centuries. There is also an attractive wetland where the undergrowth is of a very different character to the dry slopes of the ridges, yet the tree planting is similar.

The winding wooded valley between Lawrence's Hill and The Wrekin is usually called the Forest Glen, as were the Pavilions, a collection of wooden huts which were for many years the hub of the area. Here were not only teas and ices for visitors in the daytime but also dinner-dances in the evenings. Daytime trippers came in the 19th century, first by train to Wellington and then by horse-driven charabanc to the Glen. Later there were motor-charabancs and the popularity of the Forest Glen Pavilions survived into the late 1980s when the owners, the Pointon family, finally gave up. One of the wooden buildings has been taken to Blists Hill museum to be re-erected, the remainder was reduced to rubble. One of the major local mysteries for many years was how such a great atmosphere could be generated in such decrepit buildings.

There are still people in the Black Country who come for a walk up The Wrekin, though now most come in their own cars. For several generations it was a tradition to come here on holiday at least once a year. The expression, to go 'all round The Wrekin', meaning to take a circuitous route, is well known in the West Midlands, even by those who have very little idea where The Wrekin is. This is probably because there was a good deal of emigration from the industrial

Yew tree ridge.

Old postcard of Forest Glen Pavilion.

areas of East Shropshire to the West Midlands last century and the love of Shropshire's favourite hill has been passed down the generations.

All that remains at the time of writing is a small pile of rubble and plans for a new building, less idiosyncratic but far more solid and hygienic, a modern pub/restaurant with accommodation. Perhaps this will develop its own atmosphere. There are also memories of functions; Freemasons, Police Balls, Plumbers', Council dinners and so on. During wartime rationing there would be 'Wrekin Fox' on the menu, meaning whatever meat could be obtained, and there was 'Forest Glen Pudding', always Christmas pudding whatever the time of year. A local joke was to ask any couple leaving a dance early if they had their fern tickets. Here was usually the Wrekin Toast after dinner, to 'All Friends Around The Wrekin', and ending 'and may the Devil rain pebblestones on the toes of our enemies, so that we may know the buggers by their limp'.

The Forest Glen Pavilions were set up in the last century to cater for the increasing tourist trade. It is difficult in these days of foreign holidays to realise that there was a time when a holiday meant literally a day, a day out, probably by train or on foot, to a nearby beauty spot which had become famous for some reason. Here food and drink would be provided for the energetic holidaymakers who flocked to The Wrekin for exercise and fresh air.

In time the business expanded to provide accommodation for the dinner-dance fashion of the middle of this century, opening in the evenings as well as providing for the daytime trade. The functions were run by various clubs and organisations, not by the proprietors. The buildings were wooden and the plumbing rather primitive, but that did not deter dinner jacketed diners from enjoying themselves. The Pointon family, 'Ossie' and his son 'Percy' with their families lived in a bungalow next to the pavilions and provided the basic organisation. They had accumulated a marvellous collection of china, mostly Coalport, which was on display in the main dance hall. This has now gone to the museum at Coalport.

The food provided for a dinner dance, a party or a wedding reception was always first class and well cooked but rarely varied in menu. Those few guests who were allowed to stray into the kitchen were always amazed at the spartan facilities with which the cooks coped and always managed to produce hot food on time. Hardly surprisingly when the Pointon dynasty ran out, so did the Forest Glen. There were valiant attempts to recreate the atmosphere but in the end the old buildings were allowed to deteriorate and moulder, leaving vandals to set fire to them. Finally they were demolished in 1991 and as I write we await the buildings of a new restaurant to take its place.

A grey wagtail nests every year in the quarry by the Forest Glen and in May and June can be seen carrying food to its young in the rockface of the quarry.

A stream runs down the valley from the Willowmoor, of which more later. Alongside this brook are some interesting slope changes suggesting roads other than the present one, and that at some time the stream has been dammed, perhaps to power a mill, though I know of no records of a mill closer than Cluddley. A tributary comes down from a small valley between The Wrekin and Hazel Hurst, an interesting ridge to the southwest.

Here indeed are hazels in plenty, a very useful plant for centuries. The hazel provides nuts in season and its twigs are valuable for walking sticks, fencing, and handles for tools, whilst thinner twigs made the wattle for wattle-and-daub walls. It is now much rarer than it was in medieval times, for then it was extensively planted as underwood, coppiced every 12 years. Hazel Hurst has recently been coppiced and replanted with broadleafed trees. There are several old roads and stream crossings but because the fields higher up are fenced off with barbed wire the tracks go nowhere. Perhaps because of this there are few visitors and wildlife is more abundant here than in more popular places. On a recent visit an owl nearly collided with me as it flew silently past.

Hazels have been in this country for over 10,000 years; long before the English Channel and the Irish Sea were formed. They must have been useful to the Mesolithic men who were here when they arrived and their use continues. Phil Coleburn and Bob Gibbons in 'Britain's Natural Heritage' say of the hazel, '...it was the universal fuel and craft tree. It was thought to lose its suppleness after 12 years' growth, and was usually cut small for wattle work and faggots. In the fourteenth century it was much in demand for sheep hurdles. This was the only form of energy or craft material available in most of medieval England, so the coppice was a sort of power station-cum-DIY shop.'

The stream, which was formerly known as Stonybrook, fills the Wrekin Reservoir just north of the Forest Glen. This was constructed in the early part of this century to supply Wellington. As the demand increased the stream water was topped up by pumping from the sandstone aquifer at Long Lane further north into this pool. More recently the town has relied wholly on pumped water and first one and then another covered concrete reservoir was built, leaving the open pool to be used solely for fishing and wild water fowl, except for occasional extraction to supply irrigation for fields. Coot, mallard and moorhen nest here and great crested grebe were recorded. The woodland fringe contains whitethroat, willow and garden warbler, yellowhammer, linnet and blackcap; it is an excellent spot for butterflies. I once saw a rabbit's footprints in powdered snow on the iced-over water.

Catkins in Hazel Hurst.

SECRETS OF THE WREKIN FOREST

Chapter Five

STEERAWAY, LIMEKILN WOOD, MADDOCK'S HILL & WILLOWMOOR

A T THE top of Limekiln Lane lies the little settlement of Steeraway. It consists of only four houses and a farm now, though years ago it must have been considerably bigger. If you drive a car up the lane, second gear is recommended.

Looking towards the south, at the top of Limekiln Lane, the Short Woods are on your left and Limekiln Woods on your right. Though these are ancient woodlands they have been the scene of industry for a very long time and are quite different from the Ercall and Wrekin woods. Below the surface are carboniferous rocks containing coal, ironstone, fireclay and limestone, all of which have been exploited over the years. This industrial activity has left its mark on the land and its vegetation, which has been described as palaeotechnic landscape. In places where the plant cover has been disturbed the forest has gradually crept back, recolonising its old haunts and healing its wounds. The result is resurgent forest, a most fascinating diversity of habitats.

On the left of the rough lane the fields have been mined for coal, earlier by very ancient methods and later as opencast. The first mines were bell-pits, dug simply into the ground and from the initial excavation the seams of coal were worked as far as it was judged safe to do so. When all possible was obtained from this seam lower seams were worked until the miners decided they had exhausted the pit's capacity. They then dug another pit nearby and began again. To get down the mine and, importantly, up again, a ladder was enough to begin with, though as it was deepened it was necessary to have some sort of pithead gear - a wheel and rope. Coal was brought up the same way. Some of the shafts were lined with wooden supports, and some of them were filled in or capped after use, though there was no thought for marking them on maps.

These old mine workings were quite shallow and the equipment for working was unsophisticated. They were simple backyard pits which could be operated by a few men and required a minimum of capital. What these men would have thought of the massive earth-moving equipment of the modern open-cast mine is difficult to imagine. Some of the old bell-pits which were unearthed were much newer than was expected; it seems they date from the

Steeraway Farm and Short Woods.

Limekiln.

depressions and strikes of the 1920s and 1930s. A later version of this mining technique was by leaving pillars of coal to hold up the roof while extracting the coal from between them - the 'pillar and stall' method. Wooden props in places were used instead of leaving the pillars, thus enabling more of the coal to be removed. Either of these methods enabled the miners to work further away from the shaft than was possible without some kind of support for the roof. As this area is on the west side of the coalfield, where the coal seams are relatively near the surface, the shafts were not of great depth and so the methods used could be simple, cheap and unsophisticated.

There are records to show that in the early 19th. century the Lawley Company, who made iron just across the Dawley Road, paid royalties on the following: Clod Coal, Sulphur Coal, Thick Coal, Pennystone Ironstone and Loam. These were paid in 1824 by James Clayton, the agent, to the Forester estate.

Some of the earlier colliers were entirely free-lance but later the organisation was taken over by charter masters who paid rent and royalties to the landowner, sold the coal, iron, limestone and clay, and paid wages to the miners. At times the charter masters made a good profit which some invested in property to be rented to their employees and others. When coal prices were depressed, however, it was the workmen who found themselves without wages.

The open-cast working took place in the 1970s and several hundreds of thousands of tons of coal were excavated and carried off to the power station at Buildwas. This was a much more extensive and capital intensive operation. The giant earth-moving machinery dug an enormous hole over 500 feet deep below where the fields now are. A concrete road, which has since been removed, was carved through the woods to New Works and huge trucks carried out the coal. The overburden was piled on the west side of the road, to be eventually replaced. Reportedly this was a successful and cost-effective operation, but the fields will never again be as full of wildlife as they were before. They must, however, be safer; cows had been known to disappear down shafts on this land.

Within the eastern fields there was an isolation hospital which fell out of use as the diseases which were isolated there became capable of being cured and later eliminated. This is one old building which was destroyed with no regrets by anyone. The last remnants were swept away by the open-cast working.

So there is now no coal between Limekiln Lane and the ridge to the east which here forms the skyline, but there are plans to attack the rest of the area, between this ridge and the Dawley Road as far south as Lawley and Huntington, described in the next chapter. The Short Woods themselves, although having coal beneath them, together with similar ancient mines, have been spared British Coal's attentions, mainly due to their value as a wild-life reserve.

Just to the south of the point where the track becomes a footpath now are a pair of well preserved limekilns. These were in use within living memory. They are difficult to find, especially when the leaves are on the trees, for they have been overgrown during their many years of disuse. The kilns are built of solid stone into the side of the hill so that they could be easily filled from above and emptied below. Their function was to burn limestone, mined in the woods, using coal as fuel. The burnt lime was known as quicklime, a dangerous substance which had to be treated with the utmost caution. Quicklime was then watered and it became slaked lime, which was widely used as a dressing for fields. At one time there was a light railway from here to the Holyhead Road in Wellington. The firm operating these kilns included Richard Groom, the timber merchant, and the Ison family who were grocers in Wellington.

Most, if not all of this land, was owned for several generations by the Forester family of the Old Hall, later of Dothill and still later of Willey Park. It seems likely that the mining and limeworking were subject to royalties but by the time the fifth Baron sold the land there was little profit in it.

From Steeraway to the south-west is, or rather was, a rich seam of Carboniferous limestone, extremely pure and ideal for industrial purposes. There is now little left at a level which would be convenient for exploitation. How long this seam has been mined is not known but probably some small part was used in the early Iron Age. From then on there was quarrying and mining until the first quarter of this century.

The limestone was used as a flux for iron working. There are some iron ores which do not need additional limestone as they are self-fluxing, that is having enough lime in the ore. That these deposits were used in iron-smelting is certain, for a light railway ('ginny rail') led from Steeraway to Horsehay works; part of the track is still used as a footpath. Another similar ginny rail took limestone to Lawley Furnaces to the east. Limestone was added to the iron ore and coke in the furnace, which was fired and produced molten iron and slag. Even in the charcoal furnaces before Abraham Darby's time limestone was used.

The flat ground in front of the limekilns is densely grown with trees and undergrowth. Above the kilns again it is flat and here is evidence of the limestone, mostly ground quite small, but with plenty of fossils - some brachiopods (shells) and many broken pieces of corals and crinoids (sea lilies). Among the crushed limestone above are lime-loving plants including some beautiful orchids.

There has been work in 1990 and 1991 to make the limekilns and their associated mines and quarries safe. A report was commissioned by the County Council, Department of the

Resurgent vegetation above limekilns.

The Miners' Well.

Environment, Wrekin District Council and Bridgnorth District Council from Ove Arup and partners in 1987, which gives an interesting account of the state of the woods and in particular the dangers of the old limestone mines left open. It is a wonder that there have not been accidents.

The Steeraway mines were featured in the report of the 1842 Commission on the employment of children. The report shows the grim and dangerous working conditions to which young children were subjected, with frequent accidents and labour problems. It was surely no accident that the mine closed soon after the report was published. We may complain about the noise and dust, the pressure on roads and the desolation of the countryside caused by modern open cast working but compared with the conditions of last century this is as nothing.

Although some of the limestone mines and adits have been capped for safety there are still relics of the limestone trade left hiding in the woods. These include the 'miners' well', a spring to the south-west of the limekilns, and at least one old adit nearby which has a narrow entrance and expands inside to a large, lofty cavern. Otherwise there are deep trenches along the line of the carboniferous limestone deposits, often exposing sandstone. As one would expect there are many lime-loving species among the vegetation, including common spotted orchids.

There are also several badger sets, some large and ancient, others dug into the limestone workings. During the open-cast mining the danger to the large badger population was recognised by the Coal Board. A temporary concrete road was built from the site to New works so that the coal could be transported without using Limekiln Lane. The mine manager helped to cut holes in the fencing along the road where badger tracks crossed it. The truck drivers were encouraged to look out for badgers, especially early and late, by the offer of a pint of beer for the first driver to spot one. The resulting interest was well worth the price of a pint!

The north-western tip of the Limekiln Wood has an old reservoir which used to supply Wellington. There are two pools, a small upper pool and a larger, lower one. These have not been used for their intended purpose since the Forest Glen reservoir was opened in the 1930s; the larger is now for fishing and the smaller often used for pond-dipping expeditions from local schools. During the open-cast operations these pools dried up but are now full again. Presumably the water table was affected by the workings and is now restored.

From the end of the Limekiln Lane lead two ancient metalled roads which are now footpaths; one to the reservoirs and the other to The Hatch. The Hatch path must have been at one time a road but there is now a stile, precluding horses. Less than a hundred yards south there is a fork, left over the fields to Lawley and straight on to The Hatch. The Lawley route

SECRETS OF THE WREKIN FOREST

often amuses walkers, who find a lone stile on its own in the middle of the field. Before leaving the woods there is a pool on the right and another called Parker's Pool a little further on.

Another path goes right from near the fork over the top of the limekilns, which have been left open and unfenced, leaving a vertical drop into the kilns unprotected. From this track is easy access to the miners' well and the addit, both in the woods to the south; it also continues to join the track from Steeraway to the old reservoirs. Unfortunately the machinery used for clearing and sealing the shafts has damaged the emerging vegetation badly, though it will presumably regenerate if left alone.

Straight ahead, towards The Hatch, the track leads between Black Hayes and the Limekiln Wood. At one point there in an adit which passes under the path; this was reported by Ove Arup as dangerous in 1987, and it was recommended that the track be diverted round it, but that seems not to have been done - yet. I am told it is possible to walk into the mine from the left, pass under the track, and climb up on the other side, but I have never been brave enough to try.

Half way along there are the remains of a gamekeeper's cottage; not much house but a well laid hedge and a few daffodils and other cultivated plants in the garden. Opposite was another cottage kept at the turn of the last century by a widow lady called Old Annie, who relied on her garden and charitable friends to keep her and her children. Somewhere near here is the site of a very harrowing tale by Hesba Stretton (Sarah Smith) the Wellington best-selling author whose 'Jessica's First Prayer' sold a million and a half copies. The story is of a terribly poor woman who suffered many traumas but kept her faith that God would reward her in the end; like most of Hesba Stretton's work it was published by the Religious Tract Society in the latter half of last century.

From a little further along the deep trench seems better organised and more recent. It will be from here that the limestone came for the Hatch Kiln, together with an extension past The Hatch towards The Willowmoor. There are also old mine workings on the left of the path. Here, surprisingly, are planted ornamental trees, including some beautiful beeches and a few pines.

West of the limestone workings Limekiln Wood is very different. This is partly because it has not been worked and the vegetation is less disturbed and partly because the underlying rock is sandstone. Here the wood is much more open, mainly of oak and birch, with rowan, holly and other smaller trees, except for a small patch which was planted with larch, presumably for pit props. Here was recently a man nicknamed Jungle Jim, living as a squatter; perhaps he is still there.

The open nature of much of Limekiln Wood makes it attractive to birds and small mammals

Entrance to limestone adit mine.

Old reservoir, LImekiln Wood.

and because it has not been managed or tidied up there are enough dead trees and branches for insects and those who live on them. There is a small stream which rises in the middle of the wood and flows northwards to fill the old reservoirs. Some of this wood can reasonably be called semi-natural ancient forest, other parts are resurgent post-industrial habitat. Consequently it is species-rich and a fascinating field of study for ecologists.

Golf Links Lane begins in Wellington on the Holyhead Road next to Hollybush Farm, at one time a coaching inn, which gave its ancient name - Hollybush Lane - long before there was a golf course. This must have been, like Limekiln Lane, a very old route from Wellington through the forest and probably continuing towards the ford across the river at Buildwas. It now becomes interesting just after it has crossed the M54 by an underpass. Here the golf course is on the left and the Ercall woods on the right, beyond the old meadow mentioned previously. There is a right of way which begins near the underpass and goes to the left between the M54 and the course, follows the hedge to the right and leads to the limekiln pools.

A little further up the road the golf course crosses and there is a new road to the club house, diverted from the old lane which now becomes a bridleway. Just here it is deeply cut into the rock, giving a hint of its probably pre-historic origins. Limekiln Wood is now on the left and there is a path to the old reservoirs - often very muddy indeed.

The track continues to the south until it comes to the site of the New House Farm, at one time called the Dormy House, which is now demolished and all traces removed. Here the right of way crosses the golf course and heads for the edge of the trees on Maddock's Hill along a slight ridge, turning right towards the south again, between the trees and the golf course. There are good views of the Ercall, Lawrence's Hill and The Wrekin across the fairways and many interesting small trees lining the track. Maddock's Hill quarries extended across the way and the track has been diverted; it now curves to reach the Forest Glen - Huntington Lane, blocked to vehicular traffic by huge boulders of Camptonite but easily passable on foot.

Just up the lane to the left is the Hatch, which is an abandoned cottage, once a small holding with its associated sheds, all on the south side of the road from the Forest Glen to Huntington. The farm was abandoned in the 1950s when new regulations for water supply made it impossible to produce milk there without the great expense of piping water from a considerable distance. Near the cottage is a fascinating patch of fungus. Here was once a limekiln which was operating mainly during the last century and quarries and mines from which the limestone was extracted. A tongue of woodland extends to the south hiding the long deep ditch of a quarry.

There is a right of way on the west side of this wood, approached to the left of the derelict shed. It skirts between the quarry and the open fields on the right and is a most interesting walk, with varied plant cover and excellent views of The Wrekin. The quarry is deep and steep, full of trees which have regenerated naturally and lime loving plants. There is evidence of a large badger population. At the end of the wood the path arrives at a stile and crosses the fields for a couple of hundred yards to the Little Wenlock road. A similar distance down this road to the right is a right of way through the edge of Wenlock's Wood which crosses the lane to Wrekin Farm and joins the southern perimeter track on The Wrekin.

The Willowmoor area poses a host of questions for archaeologists. There were, until Victorian times, a very large number of burial mounds - tumuli - of Bronze Age dates. There are few signs of this any more, for many of them were roughly excavated and robbed by some sort of enthusiast in the last century. The grave goods which were found were treated in much the same way as the Victorians treated other finds - they were sent off to museums in various places. Some are at Shrewsbury, others in Birmingham and I understand that there is even part of the Willowmoor Hoard somewhere in the United States. This fragmentation of the evidence makes it impossible to have much idea what sort of people lived here, when, and what they did.

It is unfortunate that early archaeologists destroyed most of the evidence which would have shown us how our Bronze Age ancestors lived. It is also unfortunate that farmers have since ploughed over most of the remaining traces of pre-history here. Old maps show many tumuli in the fields around the Willowmoor farm, modern maps show far fewer and there is very little to see on the ground.

In a field near Hazel Hurst is a small cache of even more ancient artifacts. These are stone axes which have come from the 'axe factory' on Corndon Hill in the south Shropshire/Powys borderlands. The stones must have been brought here, presumably by traders, probably three thousand or more years ago. There has been some investigation of the Corndon Hill area by Frank Noble in the 1960s, He found evidence of specialist stone shaping activity. It is a hope that one day there may be some study of the Willowmoor area by a properly trained team - yet perhaps not, for these investigations are normally only conducted when there is a threat of serious damage being done to a site. Enough damage has already been done!

Hazel Hurst, to the north of the Willowmoor fields is a ridge leading from the road up to The Wrekin. It has a similar ecology to the Orleton woods further north, from which it is mostly separated by small fields. The difference in the woodland is that it has been recently coppiced and replanted. The owner - not Orleton estate - seems to have taken some of the timber. This may well have been beneficial to the bird population. There is only a short right of way, and

The Dairy Pit.

Maddock Hill quarry with geology students.

that goes nowhere. Access at the top of the wood is restricted by wire fencing around the fields.

On both sides of the Forest Glen valley are streams, all of which flow northward into the reservoir. A look at these streams repays thought, usually with questions. On the southeast is a deep valley containing a stream which begins in the fields. Here can be seen several odd looking changes of slope, including one which looks as if it were part of a dam across the stream for a millpond. Yet I have never heard of a mill here.

This stream crosses under the road and is joined by another which comes down from the side of Hazel Hurst. There are several pointers to previous works, including one place where the stream divides into two for no obvious reason. There are also traces of old roads or tracks on the opposite side from the existing road and at least one cart track crossing to the fields. Most of these interesting anomalies cannot be seen except when the vegetation has died down for the winter, so any visitor who does not like being puzzled had better look at it in high summer. The stream itself flows into the reservoir and then on to become the traditional boundary for Wellington. It was once called Clerkenbrook and flows northwards for some way with several names including Cludley Brook, Orleton Brook and Bean Hill Brook before joining the Tern. At this point the water turns south-west on its way to join the Severn.

Maddock's Hill is actually the second highest hill in the Wrekin range, being just a little higher than The Ercall. But now an enormous amount of Maddock's Hill has been quarried away for the hard core needed to make the foundations for Telford New Town. It is the price we have had to pay for a decision made in Whitehall with no effective local participation. There had been permission for a small quarry long ago, the sort of operation requiring a few men with picks and shovels and a horse and cart. Looking at old maps it is clear that the contours of the quarry did not change much over many years before the advent of Telford, when suddenly there was the demand and the money for modern earth moving equipment and techniques. The rock removed was Camptonite, a hard brown crystallised rock which was intrusive into the Shineton Shales. As Peter Toghill says in his 'Geology in Shropshire' (published by Swan Hill), "At Maddock's Hill the dip of the green-brown shales is almost vertical and they have been intruded by a late Ordovician rock called Camptonite, rich in pink feldspar and green pyroxene and hornblende. In a simple classification of igneous rocks this would be termed a microdiorite. The intrusion, although vertical, is parallel to the bedding and thus is a sill, in contrast to a dyke, which cuts across the bedding. The sill is about 80m thick but can only be traced 800m in a north-east - south-west direction." The Camptonite is an interesting rock to look at, as it contains large crystals what Toghill calls an ophitic texture, large pyroxene crystals containing smaller crystals of feldspar which give the rock its strength and thus make it useful for roadstone.

The Shineton Shales are well exposed, thanks to the quarrying. Toghill points out that they were named after the village of Sheinton, but retain an old spelling. They are of the Cambrian period, a greenish brown greyish colour, and are slightly baked by the intrusive action for up to 20m on each side. These shales contain fossils of trilobites and a type of many branched graptolite; from this evidence it is deduced that the shales were below sea level when they were formed.

The quarry itself is a deep, steep defile cut like a fatal scar into an otherwise bland hill surrounded by trees and topped by grazing land. The resurgence of the forest vegetation is gaining pace since the quarrying was discontinued and the site made safe and sowed with some of the plants which grow there now. It is only fair to say that Johnson's Quarries have done their best to encourage regeneration.

Between the Limekiln Wood and The Ercall lies the Wrekin golf course on land which was previously farmed, much of it as part of New House Farm. Before then, of course, it was part of the forest, though presumably there was grazing throughout many hundreds of years. Over most of the course are fairways and greens, so there is very little natural about the vegetation, but between there are small areas of trees which have been allowed to remain. These, together with the open nature of the course, and the fact that it is ringed by trees, contribute to the wide variety of bird life which is often seen here.

The club house is only a few years old, as it was built to replace an earlier one which was in the way of the M54. Presumably the club profited by this move. From here there are excellent views in most directions, particularly over the course towards The Wrekin and down course over Wellington to the North Shropshire Plain.

Golf Links Lane is a favourite walk, where the views are broader and more open than in most parts of The Wrekin Forest. Though not a golfer I do know that the course makes pleasant scenery and I understand that it is a particularly popular course with a long waiting list for club members. In winter there is an excellent tobogganing slope just north-west of the point where the track crosses the course. Naturally it would he both dangerous and antisocial to trespass on the fairways when they are being used, which is most of the time in good weather. It is also strongly advised to look carefully before crossing on the right of way - golf balls are hard!

Golf course, looking towards Wellington.

Chapter Six

SHORT WOODS, BLACK HAYES AND THE ISOLATED WOODLANDS

THE SHORT Woods is a very strange place. Superficially there are oaks, birches, hollies and the usual undergrowth of the rest of The Wrekin Forest, but underneath it is very different. What you see masks an underground world of ancient and not so ancient mining.

The last mine here continued in use long after the other mines in the area had closed. This was a drift mine or adit which went in at such a gentle slope that lorries were backed down the tunnel to be filled with coal and were driven off to deliver the fuel to households in the Wellington area. This was until the 1950s, when the only other pit in Shropshire was the large Granville mine at St. Georges.

When almost all the coal mines in Britain were nationalised there were a very few small pits which were thought to be hardly worth the trouble of nationalising, and the Short Woods mine was one of them. The National Coal Board had little use for such a mine as this, so it was left to be worked out by its private owners.

In the end the Coal Board did buy the land, and British Coal own it now. The problem was that, some time after all the coal had been won and the pit closed, there were a series of underground fires. Walkers on the public footpath noticed smoke rising from the undergrowth. It smelt of coal. They reported it but nothing was done.

Later someone noticed flames. Bracken began to burn. Then it rained and all was quiet for a time. But there was more smoke, followed by flames and it went out again. This went on for some time. Each time there was an official investigation the fire went out. Vandals were blamed, though it could not be proved. Every now and then some remedial action was taken, which was usually successful for a time.

At various times in the 1970s, 1980s and 1990s there have been investigations and proposals for remedial action in this area. During one trial a bulldozer driver was crossing the field to the east of this wood when the front of his machine suddenly dipped. The driver went smartly into reverse, stopped, and went to look into the hole which had opened up. With a colleague he went down and saw, stretching away in all directions, a succession of stall and pillar mining. Subsequent drilling by British Coal has established that this is the situation under the Short Woods; the whole wood is

Path from Black Hayes to Short Woods.

Flash pool in Black Hayes.

completely undermined, with all the coal removed except for the pillars. Occasionally it sets on fire. This will continue for the foreseeable future unless it is treated. The amount of coal in the pillars is just about enough to pay for opencast mining of the woods, after which the land will be safe. Consequently it was proposed that the woods should be cleared and made safe as most of the surrounding farmlands are being treated.

There was, however, a great outcry, for these are ancient woodlands, the haunt of badgers, birds and others deserving of public support. It seems strange perhaps that the least economically useful places are thought to be the most deserving of our support, but that is what has happened, and it has been decided that the Short Woods will be preserved.

The northernmost corner of the woods used to have a fine stand of holly trees from which many local people collected berries at Christmas, but unfortunately, in spite of attempts by the opencast miners to protect them the whole stand slid into the huge hole and has been lost.

Near the site of the road, which has been removed and dropped into the site hole, is a spring which gushes with 'ochre water'. This is water polluted with natural iron ore, giving it a rusty appearance. This deposit used to be employed for 'raddling tups', that is marking the front quarters of rams so that they would leave their mark on the ewes as they were served. In this way farmers would know which ewes would be lambing. Nowadays colour marking is used and the likely date of the lambing of each ewe can also be estimated.

Towards the south the Short Wood fades into Birch Coppice and Black Hayes. Birch Coppice extends towards New Works in the east. It is an area of resurgent woods with open glades grazed by cattle. There are many small pits, most of which are filled with water. Some of these are actual mine shafts and others are flashes - areas where the ground has sunk due to the props rotting or the mine galleries collapsing for other reasons. Most of Birch Coppice has been mined at one time or another, and it is a collection of 'humps and hollows' being recolonised by the forest. There are two opinions about its worthiness; one says it is only rough scrub of no value for anything, but the other view is that this is a fascinating ecological development which should be studied.

The air carries seeds and scientists talk of the 'seed rain' which is constantly there to replenish the earth and to colonise any empty space. 'Nature abhors a vacuum'. There is also the stock of seeds in the soil or in any material which gradually becomes soil, and those carried by birds and animals. Between them these three sources will cause a resurgence of natural vegetation anywhere; what actually develops is a result of many factors including the microclimate. Post-industrial vegetational resurgence is becoming an interest to many ecologists; I only hope they can make their view sufficiently popular to have an influence on public opinion in time to persuade the authorities not to destroy their sources of study.

The latest proposals for open-cast mining involve land on the east side of the woodlands, mainly farm land but some of it woodland. There are a very large number of pitfalls, over eighty shafts and a dozen adits, most of which are not safe. The proposal involves stripping all the soil and vegetation off, taking out the coal - 1,800,000 tons of it - and replacing the topsoil. It amazes me that after centuries of mining there is so much coal remaining. The ground will then be safe, but sterile. Trees and pasture will be planted but it will take more than my grandchildren's lifetime for the wildlife to return to anything like the abundance of species it has now.

The land to be mined includes a Site of Nature Conservation Importance, a Prime Site of Nature Conservation Importance, some Ancient Woodland and part of the Area of Outstanding Natural Beauty. All this important and beautiful natural scenery will be stripped and obliterated. The plants and most of the animal communities will be killed. One wonders what is the point of designating land with such grand titles when desecration like that proposed is to be allowed - if it is.

On completion of the mining there is to be farmland in the north and south of the area while the central part will be for leisure use. This includes tree planting, a hotel and chalet complex, a horse riding centre and a camping and caravan tourist site. There are also to be a History of Mining Trail, an activity centre, a public house with visitor centre, some residential development and two ponds.

This land to be dedicated to leisure will, unless it is a failure, attract a large number of visitors, some of whom may appreciate their surroundings. It is bound to affect wildlife, which has had a pretty good time there until now, being largely left alone. The badgers, foxes and birds on the site now will have to move, presumably further into the woods; these are already occupied and fights are bound to occur.

Wellington Civic Society's report on the proposals concludes, "The best policy for this area is to allow and encourage it all to return as naturally as possible to the wild woods. This will take a long time. It is not a dramatic solution but the right one." Perhaps it will be heeded.

Conservation should be about controlling human animals. There is no need for most of the management schemes which are advocated; they usually have the effect of maintaining an unnatural landscape and inhibiting the wild plants and animals which would inhabit the area given a sporting chance. Yet the grazing of these woods produces attractive open glades.

Black Hayes lies just east of the Limekiln Wood, between the Steeraway - Hatch track and fields on the northern side; it is joined to Birch Coppice further south. Here is another of the old mining areas, a palaeotechnic landscape, partly recolonised and partly ancient forest. Perhaps it

Water-filled pit shaft.

Ladysmock in wetland.

is best described as disturbed ancient forest. Few people go there and it is dangerous to do so. To stray off the path could mean a fall into one of the many old shafts.

There are flash pools, adits, waterfilled shafts, old ginnyrail tracks and an unknown number of unmarked hidden pits. There are also oak, ash, holly, sycamore, birch, rowan, hawthorn, blackthorn and a small plantation of larch. Some of the ground cover is bramble or bracken but there are bluebell patches, wild garlic, grasses, most of the common wild flowers and climbers like ivy and honeysuckle. In one place there is a badger set where coal has been dug up - a badger's coal mine!

Like much of the ancient part of the forest this is a haven for birds, especially the edges and thinner parts of the interior. In May and June willow and wood warbler, redstart, pied flycatcher, tree pipit and many other species of birds, are busy collecting food for their young. Blue, great, coal, marsh and willow tits nest, along with the commoner blackbird, songthrush, treecreeper, nuthatch and others.

Butterflies of several varieties abound here, along with a large number of beetle species, dragon flies, mosquitoes (some rather aggressive); most of the more common insect species are to be found. But finding these little gems - or sometimes pests - depends on looking, listening, smelling and keeping still and quiet. You will see more if you take a stool than if you take a motorbike! 'The faster you go the less you see', is a useful motto here as in many places.

The most numerous species of wildlife, however, have not yet been mentioned. Millions and millions of creatures have been hard at it for millions of years, working unseen and unthanked at the tasks of turning rock grains into soil, nourishing plants, transforming dead animals and plants into humus for recycling. These are the aerobic and anaerobic bacteria, without which the rest of us could never survive. Perhaps we are not likely to bring a microscope powerful enough to see them, but we should at least spare them a thought.

When developers like British Coal are asked to produce an environmental impact study it never seems to occur to anyone to ask about this most basic piece of the ecology. Even the report of the British Society of Soil Science conference, held at Harper Adams College in 1988 which discussed 'Telford, a case for soil development' does not have even one mention of any of the micro-organisms in the soil. This learned society must know far more about the effects of bacteria on the soil than I will ever know, yet even they, and in the place of publication of an early essay on the uses of bacteria ('Bacteria Bunkum by Boutflower'), say nothing. We will be different; we will acknowledge our tiny helpers, some of whom must have been our distant ancestors, and say 'Thank you' for their work.

Apart from the Steeraway-Hatch track there are some footpaths in the area of Black Hayes,

Short Wood and Birch Coppice. One starts from Steeraway and goes through the farm yard into Short Wood. It is along this path that there have at times been seen underground fires. Curving through the woods, past the site of the last adit, this bridleway goes through a gate and across two fields to New Works Lane and across another field to Dawley Road opposite Lawley Furnaces.

Another path starting just above (south) leaves Black Hayes at a gate and stile and across the fields to Short Wood. In Short Wood it rises steeply and muddily, crosses a corner of a field and enters Birch Coppice. Here it divides, comes together and divides again, one branch leading to New Works Lane, the other towards Huntington.

Two rights of way leave the Hatch track near the site of the keeper's cottage. One skirts the woods towards New Works, though it is little used and not easily walked. The other leads due south towards the lane between The Hatch and Upper and Lower Huntington Farms. That also may be difficult to find without a Pathfinder map and a compass. The line of the old light railway through Black Hayes is easy to find even though it is not officially a right of way, though at the southern end it seems to peter out at a point where you are surrounded by pitfalls. It is not for the unwary.

THE DINGLES

To the south of The Wrekin are many small woodlands which have been protected from the incursions of agriculture by their steepness. These are the various dingles, the first and longest of which is Lydebrook dingle. The Lydebrook stream rises near The Hatch and flows past Upper and Lower Huntington Farms, below which it enters a steep wooded valley. South of Lydebrook Cottage on the Horsehay-Little Wenlock road it has been disrupted by opencast mining and south of Lower Coalmore Farm it is crossed by the new Ironbridge Bypass. Below the new bridge, near Leasows Farm is a small waterfall and the valley becomes known as Loamhole Dingle, through which it flows parallel to the Rope Walk and Jiggers Bank to Coalbrookdale.

Now most of this valley is given over to wildlife but that has not always been so. When woodlands were commonly used for pasture and timber production pigs and goats were grazed here and the wood was used for building, firewood, charcoal and many other purposes. The water was for washing and drinking and also to power mills and lower down the valley to work the bellows for the Coalbrookdale furnaces. Just above the Dale works are two pools formed by damming the stream. These supplied power for the factory from Abraham Darby's time until quite recently. There is now a footpath, partly on a board walk, which goes up the valley a little way. It was constructed with enthusiasm, expecting that it would be used by the

Loamhole Dingle.

Ironbridge Gorge downstream from Ironbridge.

large numbers of tourists now visiting the Ironbridge Gorge but it is now becoming overgrown.

One of the many uses of this dingle has been for tipping fly-ash and clinker from the power station at Buildwas. Most of this took place in the 50s and early 60s before it was discovered that the ash could be made into breeze blocks for building. The ash has polluted the stream and killed vegetation but there are birches, grasses, flowers and other plants colonising even this sterile and unwelcoming surface and a badger set has been dug into the loose material. There has been massive erosion and attempts to culvert the stream have failed.

The sides of the valley are composed of very unstable carboniferous sandstones interbedded with pebbles. At their highest points is a capping of glacial till derived from triassic sandstone, producing acidic soil which supports birch, oak and bilberry. The east side of this valley includes the notorious Jiggers Bank, which is constantly on the move - for the last sixty years that I remember - and is liable to have a new bump or hollow anywhere at any time.

There is controversy as to the past uses of the Ropewalk. One theory is that ropes were made here from local hemp, but others have it that there used to be a narrow gauge railway which was operated by a rope. During the hey-day of industry in Coalbrookdale all available woods in the area were coppiced and most used for charcoal being cut every 12 years. It is assumed that at one time the Loamhole Dingle must have been a site from which loam (clay) was extracted for strengthening sandy soils.

Along the west bank of the Coalbrookdale valley ancient woodland continues to occupy steep slopes, no longer used for charcoal but by the newly formed Green Wood Trust, based at the disused Coalbrookdale railway station. This admirable organisation recreates many traditional timber based crafts including coracle making.

Small woodlands on the western sides of the valley include The Wilderness and Captain's Coppice. On the eastern bank woods continue to the top of Cherry Tree Hill almost to Telford Town Park; there is also Oilhouse Coppice and Dale Coppice, the latter lining the steep side of Coalbrookdale from the church to Lincoln Hill overlooking the Severn. Alongside the River Severn are Lloyd's Coppice and opposite and a little higher are Ladywood and Benthall Ridge Wood. There are short walks in all of these for those who do not mind steep paths.

To the west the next group of woods include Braggers Hill, Harris's Coppice, Holbrook Coppice, Birches Coppice and Timber Wood. These are not often walked, nor is Devil's Dingle, for all its romantic name, which has been greatly altered by the development of a reservoir for the power station. There is a pleasant walk down (or up) Buildwas Lane from or to Little Wenlock. This is a very old road, the ancient ford on the Severn being probably the reason for the Cistercian Buildwas Abbey, a fine ruin. The original abbey was on the north side of the river, though there is now no trace of it.

Further west are small coppices; Hurst Coppice, Saplins Wood, The Holt, The Four Acres, The Longdole, Botany Bay and Hall Coppice. There are no public paths in any of these woods, most of which are in steep dingles falling down to the Severn.

The last of these complexes of woods lie in a series of dingles flowing down to Leighton. There are three main streams; the most easterly starts near Neves Castle and flows through Cherme's Dingle to Brockholes Bank. The main stream starts in Wenlock's Wood, flowing through Harper's Dingle and Gibbons Coppice and under Spout Lane near Spring Cottage, being joined in Morrel's Wood by a tributary from Little Wenlock via Marmers Covert. Flowing through Small Tongue it is joined by the middle stream, which rises just below the Needle's Eye, passing through the scout camp in Gibbons Coppice. At Brockholes Bank there is an old mill which was powered by this stream, flowing through The Marrys to Leighton. Here it was used to power an iron works which figured prominently in the Civil War, near the inn. There have been several dams along these brooks for various projects, though its only use now is for water supply for the Scout camp and its swimming pool.

The names of these southern woods are fascinating and descriptive. Many of them include 'dingle', and are steep little wooded valleys. Others are coppices, a name which reflects their use and the reason for their planting. Just a few are coverts, describing the modern use of many patches of woodland, as cover for game, mainly pheasants. There are no public paths and walkers would not be welcome in most of them for obvious reasons, though they are rich in wild life.

The only other significant wood to the south is Old Quarry Plantation, between Little Wenlock and Wenlocks Wood. This is what it says, a plantation in a now disused limestone quarry. Because of the underlying rock the flora is calcivorous, rather than the usual acid woodland in most areas.

WEALD MOORS

To the north there are no dingles, for there are no steep slopes. Many of the woods are on or near the Weald Moors, which for many centuries have been swamp, alder carr and open water. This land has, however, long been used; for instance there is a very ancient village site at Wall Farm, near Kinnersley, which, although often referred to as Iron Age is probably much older. Before wholesale draining was completed by the Duke of Sutherland (the Lilleshall family of Leveson-Gower), whose monument is on Lilleshall Hill, there had been small incursions over many centuries. Now the complex drainage system is maintained by the Strine Drainage Board.

Kynnersley Plantation and Weald Moors.

Town Park, Randlay Pool and amphitheatre.

Its topography has been described as like a soup plate, tipped at one side, with an upturned saucer in the middle.

When the landscape was much more natural than it is now this was a place for wildfowl and fish; it must have been a paradise for hunters and fishermen. Eels were a particularly important product, Crudgington producing hundreds of thousands each year. Now almost all the Weald Moors is rich farmland, with just a few small plantations here and there.

These woods include Long, Rodway, Sidney, Kynnersley, Aqueduct and Hinks Plantations with Cobbler's Acre, Cheswell Wood, Sheepwash and the most aptly named Osierbed Covert. All are planted woods but include alders, willows and other natural wetland species. They are in complete contrast with the steep sided dingles of the southern area.

PARKS

We have considered the dingles and the plantations; a third category of surrounding woods is the remains of the aristocratic parks, originally for deer. The one most like its original form is at Orleton. This is open parkland with large specimen oaks, now grazed for many years by cattle, with a small part set out for the local cricket club. Here King Charles I mustered his army and began the Civil War. There are coverts around the Hall, which is still a private family home.

Apley once had a large park but most of it is now built up, including The Princess Royal Hospital. The house has been demolished but some woodland remains from the gardens. This is open to the public and makes an interesting walk, though these grounds have been 'municipalised' by the Development Corporation and made extremely boring. Once designated as a Prime Site of Nature Conservation Importance they are now redesignated as the number of species present is a small fraction of its former glory. Why do they never learn? A lot of public money was spent 'managing' woods when what needed to be managed was people. Some decent paths was all that was needed. Dothill park is now almost all built up too, despite local protests.

There are some good residual woods in the north-east, particularly around Lilleshall Hall, now the National Sports Centre, especially Abbey Wood, between the hall and the remains of the abbey, Picken's Plantation and Gorse Covert, though Nutty Hills has been turned into a golf course. Further east Woodcote Hill is interesting but mainly contains conifers.

AMENITY WOODLANDS

Now to the last type of woodland to be found in the remains of The Wrekin Forest - newly planted amenity woods which are meant to enhance the landscape of Telford New Town.

There has been a great deal of planting during the building of the new town, especially along the roadsides and in parks. Most of this is very worthy and there has been a lot of it, resulting in the marketing of the town as 'Forest City'. It has been well meaning and 'Politically Correct' in the sense that few will be able to argue against it and it is most fashionable.

However, it does tend to be more tidy than natural looking. The trees are there but it takes a long time for the smaller species to colonise. Some of the trees seem to have been planted because their designer liked the species, rather than because they fitted the particular environment they are in. There are also large areas of 'green desert'; tidy grassed places, regularly grazed by mowers, which seem to have little function for man and none for any other animal. Perhaps when Wrekin Council find them too expensive to keep cutting they will be neglected and be let to grow wild and interesting.

The Town Park is a mixture of formal gardens, recolonised pit mounds, formal grass, children's playground, some ancient monuments to industrial history and various 'Good Ideas'. The latter include a transported medieval church, a mock castle and Wonderland, a series of fairytale tableaux. It is unfortunate that the resurgent vegetation of the ancient industrial areas has been removed in many places and replaced by fresh trees, leaving the small plants which had struggled for a century or so to establish themselves to start all over again.

Perhaps the day will come when it is no longer politically correct to bulldoze natural plants and replace them with imported species; when common varieties will be as well thought of as rare ones and when tidiness is as unfashionable in Parks and Gardens as it is in nature.

Along the sides of the many new roads, however, it is difficult to think of what could better be done than planting trees - of whatever kind. This has been done all over Telford in a most wholesale and enthusiastic manner. There are places where the effect is of driving through a forest. At least the tree species have been varied; the poor daffodil has been devalued by having huge areas planted with monocultures of daffodils, so overstated that dandelions seem a welcome change.

The thought of Telford without its trees, however, makes us realise how important they are, and that we should be grateful to all who planted them. Given time and benevolent neglect these tidy plantations will grow into real wild woods.

POSTSCRIPT: So now you know all the secrets of The Wrekin Forest? Oh no you don't! Nor do I, for I have only spent seventy years exploring it. There are far more sights, sounds, smells and feelings to be experienced. This place is unique and very precious; true ancient forest is irreplaceable, so please look after it, care for it and defend it - every inch.

The Wrekin from Wrockwardine Wood.

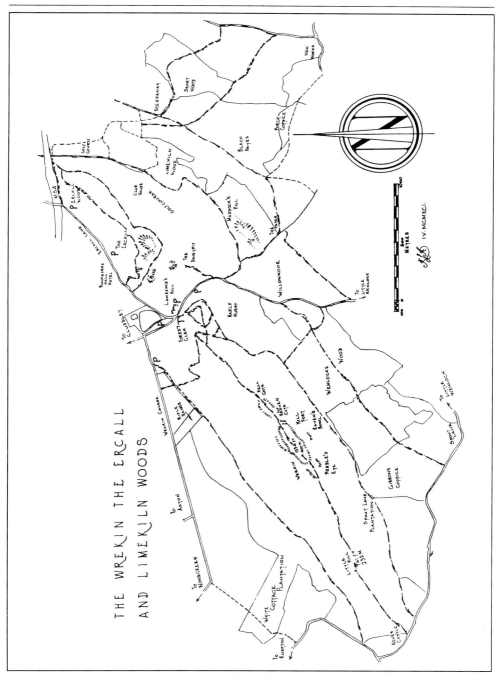

Map of The Wrekin Forest.

Grazed woodland in Birch Coppice.

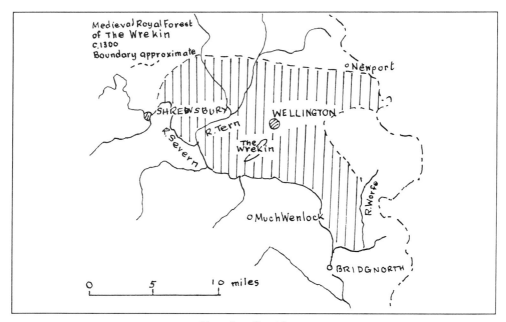

Map of medieval forest.

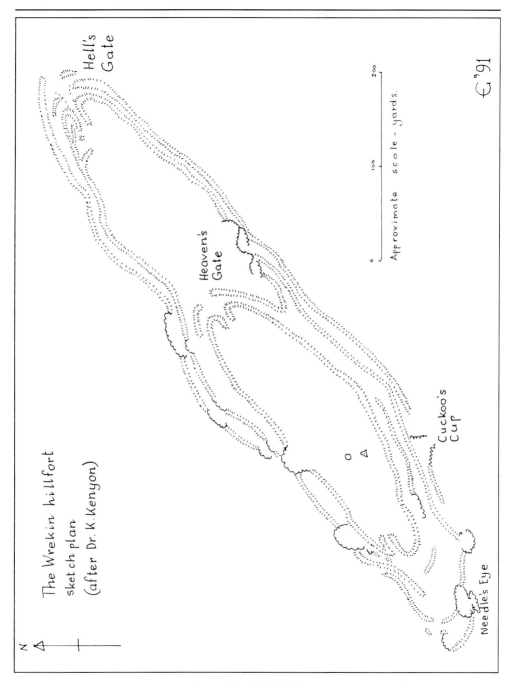

The Wrekin hillfort
sketch plan
(after Dr. K. Kenyon)

N

Hell's Gate

Heaven's Gate

Cuckoo's Cup

Needle's Eye

Approximate scale – yards.

0   100   200

G'91

Plan of The Wrekin hill fort.